INTRODUCTION

We are quite willing to enter your life for the ten or so hours you will need to read this book adequately. We have knowledge to give, and at this stage you should be a knowledge absorbing machine. In the modern music industry big and moderately big money is given to many possessors of talent and to many businessmen: who are often the same persons. Some talented persons who have trusted their business activities to others have been taken (or think they have). Since you are reading this book, we assume that you are talented. We hope that you are also smart enough to learn more about the business and legal aspects of the music and record industry.

Many organizations and companies serve various needs of the industry. We believe you should know about each such power, and have furnished you with SOME information about certain companies in this book and other books of The Entertainment Industry Series. Naturally, some organizations have detractors, competitors and/or opponents. We salute, but not necessarily endorse, all organizations whose public domain copy is reproduced in this book.

OTHER BOOKS BY THE AUTHOR(S):

The Record Industry Book
The Music Industry Book
The Publisher's Office Manual
The U.S. Master Producers & British Music Scene Book
The Movie Industry Book
The Managers, Entertainers & Agents Book
Film/TV Law (Your Introduction To Film/TV
    Copyright, Contracts & Other Law)
Film Superlist: 20,000 Motion Pictures In The
    United States Public Domain
Music/Record Business & Law (Your Introduction To
    Music/Record Copyright, Contracts & Other
    Business & Law)
Motion Picture Distribution (Business &/Or Racket?)

POSTER
The Entertainment Industry Money Flow Chart

YOUR INTRODUCTION TO

MUSIC/RECORD

COPYRIGHT, CONTRACTS

AND OTHER

BUSINESS+LAW

BY

WALTER E. HURST
and
WILLIAM STORM HALE

AUTHORS OF
"The Record Industry Book"

7ARTS PRESS, Inc.

This book is dedicated to career people: El Chicano, Kim
Fowley, Earl Palmer.

*"Every man who knows how to read has it in his power to
magnify himself, to multiply the ways in which he exists, to
make his life full, significant and interesting."*
— *Aldous Huxley*

This publication is designed to provide accurate and
authoritative information in regard to the subject matter covered.
It is sold with the understanding that the publisher is not
engaged in rendering legal, accounting or other professional
service. If legal advice or other expert assistance is required,
the services of a competent professional person should be
sought.   — *From a Declaration of Principles jointly
adopted by a Committee of the American Bar Association and
a Committee of Publishers and Associations.*

Cover and Illustrations by Donato Rico
Typography by M. Anderson
MUSIC/RECORD BUSINESS & LAW
©Copyright 1974 by Walter E. Hurst
All Rights Reserved, International Copyright Secured
Manufactured in the U.S.A.

Library of Congress No. 74–75024
Hurst, Walter E. & Hale, William Storm
Music/Record Business & Law
Hollywood, CA   Seven Arts Press
1974 June
(The Entertainment Industry Series, vol. 9)
Standard Book No. –0911370–21–8   Hardcover
–0911370–22–6   Paper

This is Volume 9 of The Entertainment Industry Series.
U.S. ISSN 0071–0695
For additional copies of this book, mail $10.00 in cash,
check or money order to:
SEVEN ARTS PRESS, INC.
6605 Hollywood Boulevard, No. 215
Hollywood, CA 90028

TABLE OF CONTENTS

CHAPTER 1

AFTRA MINIMUM RATES
COST OF A MEMBER OF AFTRA

The following minimum compensation shall be paid to artists for making phonograph recordings:

(a) SOLOISTS AND DUOS who are engaged to perform on phonograph records shall receive a minimum of $74.75 per person ($81.50 effective as of April 1, 1973) per hour or per side, whichever is higher, provided that soloists and duos who are engaged for performing on phonograph records where the terms of such engagement include any royalty payment, shall receive a minimum of $60.50 per person, per hour or per side, whichever is higher.

(b) GROUP SINGERS

No. of Singers in Group	Rate per person per hour or per side whichever is higher Effective 4/1/73	Minimum call Effective 4/1/73
3 to 8	$30.00	$60.00
9 to 16	24.00	48.00
17 to 24	21.25	42.50
25 or more (non-classical)	18.00	36.00

In the event payment on the hourly basis is more favorable to the artist, such payment may be computed in quarter-hour periods, i.e., payment shall be made on the basis of one fourth of the hourly rate for each quarter-hour or part thereof.

In addition to the above compensation each singer shall receive premium pay in an amount equal to $2.50 per hour for each hour or part thereof worked between 12 midnight and 6:00 a.m. Monday thru Friday and for all hours worked on Saturday and Sunday.

Rates are correct as of 1971-1974, but may not be correct when you read this. Write to AFTRA for the current rates.

CHAPTER 2

AMERICAN FEDERATION OF MUSICIANS

The American Federation of Musicians is a controversial
and powerful union, which negotiates contracts with employer
groups in fields of recording, live entertainment, motion
pictures, television, advertising, etc. The AFM has locals throughout the United States, the biggest locals being Local 802 in
New York and Local 47 in Los Angeles.

Theoretically, union members must work only for
employers who have executed AFM agreements. The employer-
employee contracts should be on AFM approved forms / extra
provisions may be added. Booking agents who want to book
top drawer acts belonging to the AFM, often sign contracts
with the AFM. The AFM issues booklets covering employer-
employee relations, such as Booklet B covering tours in the U.S.
and Booklet F covering foreign tours.

Union members pay annual dues to their local, and if they
work, they may have to pay work "taxes."

Employers pay the AFM money for health and welfare
funds and for pension funds. Record companies pay a Trust
Fund royalties based on record sales; the Trust Funds distribute
about half that money to musicians, arrangers, copyists, who
work for record companies and are so reported on AFM forms;
the other half is distributed to musicians throughout the
country as pay for playing without charge at various public and
semi-public events (parks, schools, hospitals, etc.).

Many musicians (including AFM members) play for
employers for cash, for a variety of motives. The employer may
want to save union fees, taxes, bookkeeping and may pay less
than scale. The employee may want to avoid paying taxes and
union fees, and may want to receive his money more quickly.
This conduct is frowned upon by the union, and the union may
punish a union member who violates the union of a local's
constitution, by-laws, rules, regulations.

CHAPTER 3

THE
ARTIST

The artist may be a solo artist (such as Bobby Womack), a duo (such as Cheech and Chong), a group (such as The Rolling Stones).

The artist generally wants to work live (dances, concerts, theatres, night clubs) for as much money as he can get.

Other things being equal, potential employers group artists as being
- (a)   no box office value,
- (b)   some box office value,
- (c)   great box office value.

CHAPTER 4

ARTIST ON THE ROAD
$ $ $ $ $ $ $ SPENDS MONEY

1. Booking Agent
   15% or 20% for 1 to 3 nighters
   10% to 15% for 4 or more nights
2. Personal Manager
   10% to 25% (he may take a reduced amount
   if an agent must be paid)
3. Musicians, Vocalists
4. Instrument, Equipment & Equipment Personnel
5. Road Manager 5% or salary
6. Transportation: Airplanes, airport limousines,
   taxis, vans
7. Accommodations
8. Food
9. Tips
10. Arrangements & Copies
11. Overhead of home office
12. Long Distance Telephone Calls for business
    and personal reasons
13. Entertainment for business & personal reasons
14. Taxes
15. Costumes (?)
16. Public Address System (?)
17. Lights (?)
18. . . . .
    . . . .
    . . . .

    and other . . . .

CHAPTER 5

ARTIST–RECORDING COMPANY
RELEASE OR RELEASE CHECKLIST

1. Does the contract provide that "If more than the minimum number of masters are recorded in one recording year, the excess number of masters recorded in that year may be applied to meet the minimum number of masters requirement of subsequent years."

    (a) If the contract does not have such a clause, give a + to the record company.

    (b) If the record company is willing to strike the provision, gave a (0) to the record company.

    (c) If the record company is unwilling to strike the clause, give five – – – – – to the record company.

2. Does the contract provide that "If Record Company fails to record the minimum number of masters in any one year, then the only obligation of company shall be to pay Artist the minimum union scale for the unrecorded masters."

    (a) If there is no such clause, mark +

    (b) If there is such a clause and it is struck from the proposed contract, mark 0.

    (c) If there is such a clause and it stays in the contract offered to you after you request its deletion, mark five – – – – –.

3. Does the contract offered to you provide:

    (a) Company may not exercise an option to renew the contract for another year unless company has recorded the minimum number of masters during the current year.

    (b) Company may not exercise an option to renew the contract for another year unless at least 2 singles have been released during the then current year.

    (c) Company may not exercise an option to renew the contract for another year unless at least 1 LP (containing at least 8 songs which were not on previously released LPs) have been released during the current year.

    For each such clause present, mark ++.

    For each such clause absent, mark – – – –.

CHAPTER 6

ARTIST'S RECORD COMPANY SELECTION CHECKLIST
+   0   −

1.   Are its headquarters in the same town in which the artist stays when he is not on the road? (For example, RCA is in New York. If the artist headquarters in New York, write a + next to RCA. If the artist headquarters where RCA Maintains a branch, write an 0. If the artist headquarters elsewhere, write a −.)

2.   Does the record company have its own big record club? If so, write +. Does the record company have strong ties to a big record club (look at what the club is offering in product and which record companies produce the product). If so, write 0. If you see one or no product of the record company released through the big clubs, write a −.

3.   Does the record company handle its own tape distribution? If so, it can pay full-rate royalties on its domestic tape sales, and can coordinate record and tape advertising-distribution. Write + if the answer is "yes" − if the answer is "no" write −.

4.   Are you dealing directly with a major record company? If so, write +. If not write −. If the company distributes its own records and has hits regularly, but is not a major, write 0.

5.   Does the company distribute its own records (+) or does it produce records on its own label to be distributed by a major (0) or does it produce masters and sell them to record companies (−).

6.   Was the company's original offer of royalties to the artist 5% or more (+), 4% (0), 3% or less (−) of RETAIL PRICE.

7.   Was the company's original offer of royalties to the artist 12% or more (+), 10% (0), 8% or less (−) of WHOLESALE PRICE.

8.   If the offer by the record company is to be a master producer, is the offer, IF BASED ON RETAIL PRICE, 10% or

more (+), 8-9% (0), under 8% (−). If BASED ON WHOLESALE PRICE, 22% or more (+), 18-21% (0), under 18% (−).

9. Is the record company paying an advance. Yes (+), No (−).

10. Is the record company paying an advance related to the amount it would have cost the record company to produce the masters the artist is giving the company at the time of signing the contract? Write (+) if the advance exceeds the cost. Write (0) if the advance roughly equals the cost. Write (−) if the advance is less than the cost.

11. Did the record company representative: (a) tell you that his company is honest? If not, write (0), if yes, write (−). (b) tell you that he is honest? If not, write (0). If yes, write (−).

12. Did the record company representative tell you that you are being paid less because that allows the company to spend more on promotion? If not, write (0), if yes, write (−).

13. How well does the record company do on the ARTIST−RECORDING COMPANY RELEASE OR RELEASE CHECKLIST?
   Well (+).   So so (0).   Badly (−).

14. Have you approached and been rejected by the record companies which appear better than the company which wants you? Write (+) if you have been rejected by more than 5 better companies. Write (−) if you have been rejected by no better company. Write (0) if you have been rejected by 1-5 better companies.

CHAPTER 7

Each year several dozen entertainers gross hundreds of thousands of dollars from recording activities and live appearances.

Let's suppose that an LP sells (net) a million copies, and that the entertainer receives royalties as recording artist (30¢), songwriter (10¢), co-publisher (5¢). His gross royalties before deductions would be $450,000.

Let's be more practical, and cut down sales (net) to three hundred thousand copies average per release, figure two releases each year, and the same 45¢ royalties per LP. His gross royalties (before deductions) would be $270,000.

If album costs for such an entertainer are computed so that in each case the deductions equal $100,000, then the first entertainer's net royalties would be $350,000 and the second entertainer's net royalties would be $170,000.

There are hundreds of recording artists who make over ten thousand dollars annually by receiving recording studio scale, possibly some artists royalties, and songwriters royalties.

There are hundreds of arrangers, conductors, and sidemen in the $10,000-$100,000 annual range in recording centers such as New York, Nashville, Memphis.

There are thousands of persons employed in the national, wholesale and retail portions of the music/record industry who enjoy annual incomes in the $10,000-$100,000 range.

Glamor may be in the creative ends of the business. Regular money is in the business ends of the business.

Some creators are talented and smart enough to be both entertainers and businessmen. In both capacities, they seek qualified and trustworthy assistance.

That way, the men who make big money may be able to keep their money.

CHAPTER 8

BMI MEMO TO AFFILIATED PUBLISHERS

BMI currently licenses about one million compositions. We are simplifying our clearance procedures to serve you better. In order to insure proper processing and payment for your works, please follow these procedures carefully.

1.   You are no longer required to submit a lead sheet or printed copy with the clearance form UNLESS the work submitted is based upon or is an arrangement of a public domain work. In such case, the clearance form will not be processed without submission of either a lead sheet or a commercial recording. With respect to other works, we do reserve the right to require that a lead sheet or other printed copy be submitted to us if we specifically request one.

2.   You no longer need to send us the white record card for each new recording of a work.

3.   Do not file a new clearance form for a work which has been previously cleared but which is being assigned or partially assigned to another publisher.

(a)   If an ENTIRE CATALOGUE is sold, proper documentation of the sale should be sent directly to me or to our legal Department.
(b)   If the publisher or writer credit for an INDIVIDUAL WORK is to be changed, we must be notified by the publisher for whom the work was previously cleared.

4.   The basis of our payments to affiliates is station-supplied logs. They identify a work by title and names of the writers. It is, therefore, most important, when you issue a license for the recording of a work in your catalogue, that you make it a condition of the license that the writers' names be indicated on the label copy.

5.   It is not necessary to file clearance forms for motion picture or television BACKGROUND scores but cue sheets for such films must be submitted. A separate clearance form is essential for any FEATURE work in the score.

6.   If a work has more than one title we must be notified of both titles even if they are very similar. If a work is cleared as "The Girl From Ipanema" and recorded under the title "The Gal From Ipanema" there may be hundreds of titles in our files between the words "gal" and "girl" and the song would not be properly identified. Where the title of a previously cleared work has been changed, please notify our Index Department by letter. If a new work being submitted for clearance has alternate titles, e.g., "Both Sides Now" and "From Both Sides Now," both titles should be indicated on the clearance form.

7.   With respect to works jointly written by BMI and ASCAP writers, the BMI publisher will not be credited with a share of performance royalties greater than the percentage interest of the BMI writers or writer. For example., if a work is written by two ASCAP writers and one BMI writer, each of whom has a 33 and 1/3% interest in the work, the BMI publisher will be credited with 33 and 1/3% of the normal publisher royalties.

Our Index Department will be glad to supply you with additional clearance forms or with forms to be used for the assignment of a previously cleared work.

CHAPTER 9

BREAKING IN

There is no one way, best way, guaranteed way. There are many people working in the industry. There are job openings all the time. Most jobs are filled by relatives, friends, acquaintances. The College For Recording Arts in San Francisco gives courses to help prepare people for record industry careers. Occasionally, courses are given on songwriter, record industry business practices, copyright in such schools as Columbia College in Hollywood and elsewhere. There are books on the industry. There are trade publications. Many persons attending courses have made friends with classmates who know of job openings.

What can you do? Get education. Learn what you can within your capability. Many entertainers wind up as recording studio engineers, music publishers, master producers. A songwriter may decide that he wants to find an honest publisher and having given up in his search, may become a publisher, then a producer of his songs, then a small record company, then a freelance promotion man, then a promotion man for a large record company, then head of promotion, then head of the company, then unemployed and looking for another niche in the entertainment industry.

Your efforts must be directed to "find a need and fill it."

Record companies constantly seek artists who can (1) record, (2) perform live, (3) write. To be seen performing live, join or create a group which is very good and constantly becomes better. To be able to play a demonstration record or tape to a prospective record company, make a demo in a recording studio. Record companies want to make money in publishing original songs; therefore record original songs.

How do you get your demos (demonstration records and tapes) to record companies? One method is to walk them in yourself.

ALWAYS HAVE SAFETY COPIES OF ANY DEMO YOU
LEAVE OR CARRY AROUND. EXPECT EVERY DEMO TO
BE LOST! If you lose your only copy of any tape, tough!!!

Return to wherever you left any demo in order to get it
back. Leaving demos around may cause you to later suspect
that your song was pirated.

If you want a job in a record company — ask for it. If any
job is available (e.g. shipping clerk), take it. Discovering that a
shipping clerk is truly a potential great artist is the kind of
discovery executives dream and boast about. How you play
your game, after you have a job in a record company, is up to
you.

If you belong to any minority or group, let fellow group
members know you exist. Groups: Women. Youngsters. National
background. Religion. College. Fraternity. Locality, etc. That
and your potential ability to return the favor, may cause a fellow
group member to help you.

We suggest you obtain as much child labor (labor while you
are young) experience as you can, even if you are paid your
total worth for your time (quite possibly the amount may be $0)
in (1) performing, (2) retailing, (3) presenting shows, (4) radio
and TV — and performing wherever possible in private and in
public.

Please remember in any job interview, that the interviewer,
no matter how he may dress or talk, is looking for a reliable
person.

If there are so many jobs and momentary job vacancies in
the record industry, if record companies are constantly searching
for artists and songwriters, why is it so hard to break in?

Possibly because there are so many applicants who know
more and are better connected.

CHAPTER 10

BUSINESS INFORMATION

1. Select any entertainer you wish. Identify by name (a) the record company he records for, (b) songs he has written, (c) a publishing he owns, (d) other artists he produces, (e) a national promoter he has worked for, (f) a college at which he has appeared at, (g) his lawyer, (h) his secretary, (i) a hotel he has stayed at, (j) his musical instruments, amplifiers, and p.a. equipment, (k) his car or bus, (l) airlines he has used, (m) his booking agency, (n) his personal manager.

2. Now to some planning for yourself. Fill in the following show business information about yourself.
(a)   The record company you work for.
(b)   Songs you have written.
(c)   The publisher(s) of your songs.
(d)   Any artists you produce.
(e)   Any promoters you have worked for.
(f)   Any clubs or other locations where you have worked.
(g)   Your lawyer.
(h)   Your secretary.
(i)   Hotels where you stay.
(j)   Your equipment.
(k)   Your automotive transportation.
(l)   Airlines you use.
(m) Your booking agent(s).
(n)   Your personal manager(s).

Please don't acquire relationships with anybody just to fill in blanks. In each case where you are considering entering into a relationship consider:

1. The personal aspects.
2. The business aspects.
3. The legal aspects.

CHAPTER 11

BUSINESSMAN – ARTIST RELATIONSHIPS

1. THE ARTIST AND/OR MANAGER
   Creates an ARTIST who can
   (a) write songs
   (b) sing
   (c) play instruments
   The ARTIST may be a single person or more people.
   The ARTIST may be partner(s) or employee(s)
   and employer(s).

2. THE ARTIST AND/OR MANAGER
   Creates a desire in BUSINESSMEN to tie in with
   the team. The desire is created if Businessmen see
   themselves making money with a necessary
   amount of work and a minimum of ulcer causing
   aggravation.

3. The ARTIST wants:
   (a) Booking Agent – to get work for the artist
   (b) Record Company – to publicize the artist and
       pay royalties
   (c) Publisher – to pay royalties
   (d) Manager – to protect the artist's ego, to
       correlate the artist's business.

4. The BUSINESSMEN want an ARTIST who:
   (a) Performs adequately on time AND is "Box
       Office"
   (b) Can consistently perform to create selling
       singles and albums
   (c) Can write hit songs regularly
   (d) Grosses more and more and more money over
       a long period of time, and grosses decent
       amounts of money all the time.

CHAPTER 12

A CONTRACT BETWEEN THE SONGWRITERS

Relatively few songwriters bother to sign any contract with each other. This chapter is going to set forth a few provisions of a possible contract. But please take heed: THERE IS NO REAL GOVERNMENT APPROVED OR INDUSTRIAL APPROVED CONTRACT IN THE MUSIC/RECORD INDUSTRY. There is no single *standard* contract, *uniform* contract, *fair* contract, that serves all potential users; contracts have titles that use the word "popular," "uniform" or "standard" merely because the writers/printers of the contracts decided to place those words into the titles.

Any contract, or contractual provision, placed in this book is here for educational purposes only, and must not be used blindly and on faith.

Try to modify each form or other contract presented to you to your circumstances. (You may not be able to do so for bargaining power reasons.)

Larry Lyricist and Carol Composer agree as follows:

1. Larry Lyricist has written the words and Carol Composer has written the music of a musical composition entitled "I AM LOVEABLE, I AM GREAT, I AM HERE."

2. Each party promises to assign no rights in the song and to grant nobody the right to use the song without prior or simultaneous written consent of the other party.

3. All rights and royalties pertaining to the song shall be shared equally, as if each party had co-written both the words and the music.

CHAPTER 13

THE COPYRIGHT ASSIGNMENT

If the songwriter filed a **Form E** in the Copyright Office in which the songwriter claimed that he owned the copyright, then the publisher may want the songwriter to also fill out the following assignment.

THE UNDERSIGNED OWNER(S) OF THE COPYRIGHT IN THE MUSICAL COMPOSITION "I AM LOVEABLE, I AM GREAT, I AM HERE," WHICH WAS REGISTERED ON FORM E ON THE FOLLOWING DATE: _____ , AND WHICH WAS GIVEN BY THE COPYRIGHT OFFICE THE FOLLOWING REGISTRATION NUMBER: _____ HEREBY ASSIGN ALL RIGHTS IN, TO AND CONCERNING SAID MUSICAL COMPOSITION TO THE FOLLOWING ASSIGNEE:

Publisher: Suite Seven Music
Address: XXXX Hollywood Boulevard, Hollywood, CA 90028

Dated: _____

Larry Lyricist
Larry Lyricist

Carol Composer
Carol Composer

The publisher should promptly send the original of such assignment and an assignment filing fee of $5 to the Copyright Office.

If the publisher fails to send such assignment promptly, and if later the songwriters assign the same song to a second publisher, then there will be a conflict between the two publishers and the songwriter. There are so many factors in such a conflict, it is difficult to discuss the factors in this brief book. It is a conflict to be avoided by all concerned.

CHAPTER 14

COPYRIGHT FOR SOUND RECORDINGS

General Information
The Copyright Law (Title 17 of the United States Code) has been amended by a recent act of Congress, Public Law 92-140, to permit copyright protection for certain sound recordings, provided that they are fixed and first published with the statutory copyright notice on or after February 15, 1972. Statutory copyright in sound recordings endures for 28 years from the date of first publication, and may be renewed for a second 28-year term. The requirements for securing copyright in such works are set forth below.

What Is A Sound Recording?
A "sound recording" is a work that results from the fixation of a series of musical, spoken, or other sounds. Common examples include recordings of music, drama, narration, or other sounds embodied in phonograph discs, open-reel tapes, cartridges, cassettes, player piano rolls, or similar material objects in which sounds are fixed and can be perceived, reproduced, or otherwise communicated either directly or with the aid of a machine or device. Sound recordings, within the meaning of this act, do not include a sound track when it is an integrated part of a motion picture.

What Is Fixation?
A series of sounds constituting a sound recording is "fixed" when that complete series is first produced on a final master recording that is later reproduced in published copies.

Sound Recordings That Are Not Subject To Statutory Copyright
By the terms of the law, certain sound recordings are not subject to statutory copyright protection.

• **Unpublished Sound Recordings.** The law does not provide for statutory copyright in unpublished sound recordings. Therefore, unpublished recordings should not be sent to the Copyright Office. Unpublished recordings may be protected by the common law against unauthorized use without any action in the Copyright Office. (As to what constitutes "publication"

of a sound recording, see item number 2 of How To
Secure Statutory Copyright In Sound Recordings.)

• **Sound Recordings Fixed Before February 15, 1972.** The
law provides statutory copyright ONLY for published sound
recordings fixed on or after February 15, 1972. The statute
specifies that this provision is not to "be construed as affecting
in any way rights with respect to sound recordings fixed before
that date."

> *Should a problem arise with regard to sound
> recordings not covered by the copyright
> statute, it may be advisable to consult an
> attorney.*

Copyright In Musical, Dramatic, Or Literary Works Recorded
• Copyright in a sound recording should not be confused
with, and is not a substitute for, copyright in a musical
composition, dramatic work, or literary work of which a
performance or rendition is recorded. The Copyright in the
sound recording relates only to the series of sounds of which it
is constituted, and protects only against duplication of that
particular series of sounds.

• For purposes of registration of claims to copyright in
musical compositions, dramatic works, or literary works, sound
recordings are not acceptable deposit copies. To make
registration for such works, copies in the form of legible
notation or text are required.

• If a sound recording is made of an unpublished musical
or literary work that has not yet been copyrighted, it may be
important to make a copyright registration for that musical or
literary work PRIOR TO the publication of the sound
recording embodying it. This may be necessary to assure
adequate protection for the musical or literary work.

> *For further information concerning copyright in works
> other than sound recordings, write to the Copyright Office,
> Library of Congress, Washington, D.C. 20559. Upon receipt of a
> request specifying the kind of work in question, the Copyright
> Office will supply information and application forms free.*

How To Secure Statutory Copyright In Sound Recordings

Three steps should be taken to secure copyright protection for a sound recording:

1. *Produce copies containing the copyright notice.* Reproduce the sound recording in copies, taking care to see that all copies bear notice of copyright in the required form and position, as explained below.

2. *Publish the sound recording with copyright notice.* Publication generally means the sale, placing on sale, or public distribution of copies of the sound recording. Performance of a sound recording by playing it, even in public or on radio or television, ordinarily does not constitute publication in the copyright sense.

3. *Register the claim to copyright.* Promptly after publication, mail to the Register of Copyrights, Library of Congress, Washington, D.C. 20559, two complete copies of the best edition of the sound recording, together with an application on Form N duly completed and signed, and a fee of $6.00.

The Copyright Notice For Sound Recordings

The copyright notice on a sound recording should appear on the surface of the copies of the recording or on the label or container, in such manner and location as to give reasonable notice of the claim of copyright. The copyright notice for sound recordings consists of the symbol ℗, the year date of first publication of the sound recording, and the name of the copyright owner of the sound recording. Example:

   1973 Doe Records, Inc.

— It is the act of publication with copyright notice in the correct form and position that secures copyright protection in a sound recording. Thus care should be taken to use the legal name of the copyright owner and to group the elements of the notice together as in the previous example.

— If copies of the sound recording are published without the required notice described above, or with a defective notice, the right to secure statutory copyright for that sound recording is lost and cannot be regained. Adding the correct notice to copies published later will not restore protection or permit the Copyright Office to register a claim.

Registration

Registration of a claim to copyright in a sound recording should be made by mailing two complete copies of the best edition of the sound recording, an application on Form N duly completed and signed, and a fee of $6.00 to:

> The Register of Copyrights
> Library of Congress
> Washington, D.C. 20559

After registration, the Copyright Office issues a certificate showing that the statements set forth therein have been made a part of the records of the Office.

- **Complete copies of the best edition.** The law calls for the deposit of two complete copies of the best edition of the sound recording as first published.

— A "complete copy" means the actual sound recording, together with any sleeve, jacket, or other container in which it was first published, as well as any liner notes or other accompanying material. Concerning copyright for any copyrightable material in the accompanying items, see Sound Recordings First Published As A Unit With Other Copyrightable Material in a later paragraph.

— The "best edition," where the sound recording was first published in several physical forms, ordinarily means a vinyl disc rather than tape; or when only tape is involved, open-reel tape, the cartridge, or the cassette in descending order of preference. Usually a stereophonic recording is considered the "best edition" as against a monophonic one. It is important to note, however, that all the editions should bear the prescribed notice of copyright in order to secure and maintain copyright protection.

- **Registration for collective recordings.** When two or more recorded selections are first published together as a collective unit (for example, in an album containing recordings of 12 songs on two discs), the entire unit may be registered as a single collective work on one application, as long as the copyright owner is the same for all the recordings in the collection. If a single registration is made in such a case, the registration will be cataloged and indexed in the Copyright Office records only under the title identifying the collective work as a whole.

If the copyright owner wishes to have the individual selections cataloged and indexed under their separate titles in the registration records, he may make separate registrations for the individual selections. Each registration requires a separate application and fee.

- **When to register.** The law requries that, after a sound recording is published with the notice of copyright, registration be made promptly.

- **Application for registration.** Application Form N is for sound recordings and is provided by the Copyright Office free upon request. Care should be taken to see that it is properly completed and signed.

- **Fee.** The registration fee is $6.00. Make the check or money order payable to the Register of Copyrights. DO NOT SEND CASH.

- **Mailing instructions.** Processing of the material will be more prompt if the application, copies, and fee are all mailed together in the same package. Special attention should be given to the preparation of the containers for the shipment of sound recordings in order to prevent damage in transit. The Copyright Office cannot accept for registration sound recordings damaged in shipment.

New Versions

Under the copyright law a new version of a work in the public domain, or a new version of a copyrighted work that has been produced by the copyright owner or with his consent, is copyrightable as a "new work." Sound recordings that are copyrightable as "new works" include compilations, recordings reissued with substantial editorial revisions or abridgments of the recorded material, and recordings republished with new recorded material.

• **Copyright in new versions covers only the new matter.** The copyright in a new version covers only the additions, changes, or other newly recorded sounds appearing in the new sound recording. There is no way to restore or secure statutory copyright protection for a sound recording that is in the public domain or for a recording that was fixed before February 15, 1972. Similarly, protection for a sound recording under an existing statutory copyright cannot be lengthened by republishing the work with new matter.

• **Works reissued without substantial new recorded material.** To be copyrightable as a new version, a sound recording must either be so different in substance from the original recording as to be regarded as a "new work," or it must contain a substantial amount of new recorded material. When only a few slight variations or minor additions of no substance have been made, registration is not possible. For example, if the only change is to reissue the same recording on tape that has previously been published as a disc, no new registration would ordinarily be in order. Likewise, if the only change is to "rechannel" mechanically the same series of sounds, a new registration would generally not be appropriate.

— Also, there may be changes in one or more of the features appearing on the label, jacket, or other material accompanying the recording which are either uncopyrightable, or would be the subject of copyright in some category other than sound recordings. In either case, such material could not serve as a basis for a new copyright as a sound recording. Examples of uncopyrightable elements are titles, short phrases, or format. Elements that may be the subject of copyright in one of the classes other than sound recordings include new literary or musical expression in legible form or new pictorial material.

• **Copyright notice for new versions of sound recordings and sound recordings reissued without new matter copyrightable in Class N.** For copyright in a sound recording to remain in force, it is essential that all published copies contain the copyright notice prescribed for sound recordings; thus, ℗ 1973 Doe Records, Inc.

— If a sound recording is a new version, a new copyright may be secured in the new matter published for the first time in the new version. To secure copyright in this new matter, the copies should bear a complete copyright notice for the new version containing the symbol ℗ , the name of the copyright owner of the new version, and the year the new version was published. If an earlier version of a sound recording was also copyrighted, it is advisable to include the year of publication of the earlier version(s).

— If a previously copyrighted sound recording is **reissued without substantial new matter** subject to registration in Class N, no new copyright in the sound recording is secured when the recording is reissued. Therefore, the copyright notice should retain the original year date. If such a sound recording is reissued with a copyright notice containing only a substantially later date, the copyright in the sound recording would probably be invalidated. If the copyright has been assigned to a new owner, the name of the original owner should be retained in the notice UNLESS the assignment has been recorded in the Copyright Office BEFORE the recording is reissued. If the assignment has been recorded in this Office BEFORE, BUT NOT AFTER, the sound recording is reissued, the new owenr may substitute his name for that of the previous owner in the copyright notice. The use of the assignee's name in the notice before the assignment has been recorded here could result in loss of the copyright.

Special Kinds Of Sound Recordings
Although most of the sound recordings to be copyrighted will probably embody the performance of music, dramas, or narrative works, the nature of what is recorded may in some instances be "birdcalls, sounds of racing cars, et cetera." Such recordings may also be copyrightable and subject to registration if the amount of original recorded material is substantial.

Sound Recordings First Published As A Unit With Other Copyrightable Material

In many cases sound recordings are first published with other copyrightable material as a unit. Examples are: discs published in jackets which contain substantial original textual or pictorial matter, and which bear a copyright notice appropriate for that material; recordings for learning a foreign language which are published in a box with manuals and exercise books; and audiovisual kits which include recordings, filmstrips, textbooks, and the like.

— With the exception of the sound recording, a combination or collection of various materials, which have been published as a unit, may qualify for registration as a "book" on Form A when both of the following conditions are met:

- The work contains a copyright notice consisting of the word "Copyright," the abbreviation "Copr.," or the symbol Ⓒ accompanied by the name of the copyright owner of the "book" and the year date of publication. Example:

    Ⓒ   Richard Doe 1973

- The notice is placed in a location that could be considered the "title page" or the page immediately following the title page. For example, where an audiovisual kit is first published in a box which bears a title identifying the kit as a whole, the copyright notice should be located on the top or on one side of the box lid.

— As an alternative to registering one claim in Class A for a published combination of various materials, separate registrations may be made for the different parts, provided that they bore their own copyright notices from the time of first publication. Separate registration in Class N must be made in every case for the sound recording.

CHAPTER 15

THE COPYRIGHT OFFICE

The Copyright Office is part of the Library of Congress which is part of the United States Government.

One of the purposes of the Copyright Office is educational. You can write to the Copyright Office, Library of Congress, Washington, D.C. 20559: "Gentlemen; Please send me a list of all the catalogs and books you sell. Please send me 10 free FORM E."

Another purpose of the Copyright Office is to provide a reliable government unit where claims to copyright can be registered.

Songwriter(s) can register song(s) by following simple procedure:
1. Fill out Form E.
2. Send $6.00 (that's the current fee) payable to Register of Copyrights.
3. Send one copy of the lead sheet.

A songwriter should, for the sake of his own office records, write a letter of transmittal.

"Dear Copyright Office: Re our song: I AM LOVEABLE, I AM GREAT, I AM HERE. Enclosed are $6.00, Form E, and a lead sheet. Please process."

CHAPTER 16

DEDUCTIONS FROM GROSS ROYALTIES

If you had a choice between $1000 in your pocket or in a stranger's pocket, which would you choose?

Your pocket, of course.

If the stranger has the choice, into whose pocket do you think the stranger wants the money?

The stranger's pocket, of course.

Then, please don't be surprised that a contract which has some paragraphs which provide that gross royalties should be computed by a record company to be paid to an artist, also has additional paragraphs which provide that there shall be deductions from those royalties. Often, in fact usually, the deductions exceed the gross royalties, with the consequence that the record company need pay nothing to the artist at royalty time.

ELEMENTS OF A CONTRACT:

PARTIES CAPABLE OF CONTRACTING:
SONGWRITER / PUBLISHER

THEIR CONSENT:

In witness whereof the undersigned hereby execute this contract.

- - - - - - - - - - - - - - - - -
(signed) SONGWRITER

- - - - - - - - - - - - - - - - -
(signed) PUBLISHER

A LAWFUL OBJECT

Songwriter's assignment of copyright to Publisher

$$SW \xrightarrow{\;©\;} P$$

A SUFFICIENT CAUSE OF CONSIDERATION:

Promise to pay half of most receipts to Songwriter

$$SW \xleftarrow{\;\$\;} P$$

ENTERTAINER'S EXPENSES
(To be carefully recorded)

Legal, Accounting, Secretarial, Office, Phone.

Publicity, Advertising.

Clothing

Home Rent or payments

Taxes

Alimony (?)

Musicians, Arrangers, Roadmen

Equipment

Instruments

Booking Agent

Food

Transportation Hotels Tips

Manager

Seems like a lot of work? IT IS! Today's entertainer is a businessman, and being a businessman is work!

ENTERTAINER'S INCOME

RECORD COMPANY } Advance on Signing.
Artist's Royalties.
Exercising of Bonus Options. } RECORDING ARTIST. } ARTIST AS:

AFFILIATED PUBLISHERS } Song Writer's Royalties. → SONG WRITER.
Co-Publisher's Share → CO-PUBLISHER.

PERFORMING RIGHTS SOCIETIES } Songwriter's Royalties → SONG WRITER.
50% of Publisher's Royalties → CO-PUBLISHER.

CONCERTS....Fee or Salary → PERFORMER.
DANCES........Fee or Salary → PERFORMER.
CLUBS..........Fee or Salary → PERFORMER.
MOVIES........Salary → PERFORMER.
TV................Salary → PERFORMER AND/OR ACTOR.

$ $

CHAPTER 17

ENTERTAINER-PRODUCER NEGOTIATIONS

ENTERTAINER-SONGWRITER
I want to be a recording artist.

PRODUCER-PUBLISHER-MANAGER
I want you to record exclusively for me.

ENTERTAINER QUALIFYING THE PRODUCER:
What is your track record?

How many masters have you produced?

How many masters have you sold?

How many of your masters have been used on records?

How many hits have you had? Please identify your hit by artist, record company and year. How big were the hits?

To which record company have you sold masters?

NOTICE: These questions don't concern the contract. These questions concern whether the artist wants to deal with the producer in the first place.

PRODUCER-PUBLISHER-MANAGER SPEAKING TO ENTERTAINER:
I want to record you.
I want to publish your songs.
I want to manage you.

ENTERTAINER QUALIFYING THE PRODUCER-PUBLISHER-MANAGER:
Do you have the men and money and ability to record me and to persuade a record company to distribute my records.

Do you have any music publishing contacts and know-how that I can't learn in 20 hours?

Do you have contacts with booking agents, publicity people, radio, television, press, national tour promoters, local employers, out-of-town employers that justify a whopping management fee?

45 R.P.M. "SINGLE" CREDITS

CHAPTER 18

GROUP BOX OFFICE TABLE

EVENT PROMOTER

    1.   Our college is having its annual — — dance. We want 7 musicians. Our budget is $300. People will come to the event no matter who plays music.

ARTIST

    1.   The ARTIST need have no box office value. However, the opportunity to play before an audience allows it to please and promote itself with:
        (a)   the employer
        (b)   the booking agent
        (c)   the public

EVENT PROMOTER

    2.   Our hotel features a trio in its DRINK-A-LOT-ROOM. We want a band that pleases customers so that the customers will return.

ARTIST

    2.   The ARTIST needs something special to slowly and steadily build up his own following so that he can count on regular return engagements.

EVENT PROMOTER

    3.   On this Saturday's show we have 6 acts direct from the entertainment capitals of the world.

ARTIST

    3.   Some of the ARTISTS may have had hit records. It's important for an ARTIST to have copies of hit records for uses as calling cards and local promotion in later years. Some ARTISTS may have records on the local playlists or sales charts.

EVENT PROMOTER

    4.   This week we present SUPER-SUPER-SUN-STAR.

ARTIST

    4.   If the ARTIST really has box office value, then the promoter may make a profit and the ARTIST may gross thousands of dollars for one night's work.

CHAPTER 19

THE HARRY FOX AGENCY

What is The Harry Fox Agency?

The Harry Fox Agency represents music publishers in connection with the mechanical reproduction of their copyrights as well as the use of their compositions for motion picture synchronization and television films and video tapes.

Mechanical reproduction? What's that?

Phonograph records, tapes, electrical transcriptions and audio tapes for broadcast and background music purposes.

Something like ASCAP — right?

Wrong. ASCAP is a performing rights society as are BMI and SESAC. A publisher assigns his performing rights to one of these societies. The mechanical right is separate and apart from the performing right. The Harry Fox Agency represents both ASCAP and BMI publishers.

What will it cost to have the Harry Fox Agency represent my publishing company?

The charge is only made on royalties collected in your behalf. For phonograph records and tapes the commission is 3½% if the gross collections in your behalf are over $25,000 a year.

If they're not?

Then the charge is 5%.

Are your charges for record and tape collections ever less?

At times, depending upon overhead and economic conditions, these commission rates may be reduced at our option.

What do you do for this percentage when a record company records one of my copyrights?

We issue mechanical agreements covering each release by each record company. Some call them record licenses.

At what rate do you issue these agreements?

You determine the rate. The present copyright law provides a statutory rate of two cents per composition per record manufactured.

What happens when a record company asks for an agreement at less than the statutory rate?

This is your decision to make. We will issue the agreements based upon your specific instructions.

After you issue the agreement, then what?

We collect the royalties in your behalf. The agreements call for payment of quarterly royalties. Most record companies account at three-month periods ending March 31st, June 30th, September 30th, and December 31st.

How soon after that do I get my royalties?

A period of 45 days after each quarter is allowed for the accounting procedures required by the companies to prepare their statements.

Then, actually royalties start coming in May 15th, August 15th, November 15th, and February 15th.

Right — if they're on time. Realistically, you must realize that there sometimes are delays.

How soon after the royalties reach you do I get my check?

As soon as possible. The statements must be checked, but we try to get them to you as quickly as we can.

Can't you be more specific?

Well, royalties received from all major record

manufacturers are distributed within a week to ten days. Sometimes, a little longer. Also, all significant amounts are sent out as soon as received.

What if I need my money immediately?

If the royalties have been received, a telephone call to the office will have your statement in the mail the same day. In fact, if you want to drop up to the office, you can pick up your check.

That's fine. By the way, what is your telephone number?

What happens if the record companies don't pay?

Our function is to collect the royalties in your behalf, and we take whatever action is necessary to do just that.

Do you mean you'll sue?

When a situation arises where it appears that legal action is necessary, we will consult with the publishers involved. At such time, at their direction, a suit may be filed.

Will I have to pay for the lawyer?

No.

Do you check the statements I receive from the record companies?

Certainly. Audits of all record manufacturers are a regular part of our service. As a matter of fact, in many cases, we distribute recoveries in a year in excess of the commission you pay for our services.

Will this cost me extra?

No.

Can I ask you to check the books of a record company immediately if I don't like the statement they sent?

Well, you certainly can ask. But you must remember that The Harry Fox Agency represents over 3,500 publishers. It would be impossible for us to audit on an individual basis.

I see . . .

Our accountants do audit companies large and small at periodic intervals.

Wherever they're located?

Yes. We send our auditors all over the United States and Canada. We have even audited in behalf of our principals in Mexico, Hong Kong, and Southeast Asia.

By the way, what territories do you cover?

The United States and Canada for the fees indicated. We also have an effective collection system in Japan through JASRAC.

Does this cost more?

Yes. The present fee for representation in Japan is 12½%, which is the standard JASRAC fee.

What about other areas?

If you have not made any sub-publication arrangement for foreign coverage through another publisher, we can arrange representation for you.

How?

We work through various foreign societies abroad. Actually, through our operation and the operation of these societies the whole world can be covered.

That sounds pretty good. Then maybe I don't have to work through a foreign publisher. Right?

There's no "yes" or "no" answer to this. Remember The Harry Fox Agency as well as the foreign societies do not act as publishers. There is no advance for foreign rights, no exploitation of the copyrights, and foreign language local recordings are not solicited.

I see . . .

On the other hand, of course, you don't have to give up fifty percent of your copyright.

Now I see why there's no easy answer.

That's right. After considering all the elements you must make your own decision.

Do you provide any licensing services except for records and tapes?

Yes. Synchronization rights.

What is that?

Well, when a copyrighted song is used in a motion picture or a TV film, a license is required, and what is licensed is called the synchronization right.

Who asks for this license?

It certainly should be the producer of the film — and generally will be. If though, he inadvertently overlooks this requirement, then, of course, a claim should be made.

How much will they pay me?

That depends upon a number of factors. The importance of the song, the importance of the motion picture, and the type of use are among the criteria.

What kinds of uses are there?

Well, you have background instrumental and background

vocal and visual instrument and visual vocal and limited use
and unlimited use and . . .

Stop! How will I know what to do?

Ask questions. Find out the EXACT use as well as the
duration of the use. Sometimes you may wish to find out the
type of rating the producer thinks his motion picture may
receive.

What difference does that make?

It may affect your quotation. If it appears the film may
receive an X rating, you may wish to charge more — or less —
or perhaps not even make your song available.

Getting back to price, aren't there any guidelines?

Really not — it's just old fashioned horse-trading and
charging what the market will bear. The producer will tell you
fast enough if your price is too high. In fact, he will probably
say so even if it's not.

Once we do arrive at a price, is that all?

No — there is another area to be considered. In the United
States, the performing societies are not in a position to license
United States theatrical performing rights. The producer will
ask you for such rights.

What do I do then?

Just add them to your synchronizing license — for a price,
of course.

Who issues the license?

This is a service regularly rendered on behalf of publishers
by The Harry Fox Agency.

How much will that cost me?

The normal commission rate is 10%.

If I want you to represent my companies, for how many years must I sign up?

There is no period of time stipulated in the authorization.

You mean that at any time I can cancel the representation?

We can't imagine why, but the answer is yes.

What steps should I take to have The Harry Fox Agency represent my music publishing company?

Send us a letter asking us to represent you. Give us the full name of your company, your performing rights affiliation, and the territories you wish us to cover.

As simple as that?

Yes. Of course, we may find that we are unable to assume representation of your company at the time, but we would always consider your request again at a future date.

Your address?

The Harry Fox Agency, Inc., 110 East 59th Street, New York, N.Y. 10022.

CHAPTER 20

HOW CAN I FIND FAME AND FORTUNE?

We can give you theory which is based on actual cases. We can point out mistakes, sometimes mistakes fatal to the career of the person who made them. We can advise you how to avoid errors and overcome obstacles.

We can't, don't, and won't give you any guarantee about anything. Show business may be for you to enjoy as a consumer, but not as a money-making participant. Ingredients of success are work, contacts, talent and luck (especially luck).

You can find fame through publicity, promotion, word of mouth, public appearances, appearances on radio, television, motion picture screens, and in other ways.

You can find fortune if you are paid enough so that your income is so much higher than your expenses that you are able to accumulate savings.

CHAPTER 21

HOW CAN I GET MONEY FROM RECORD ICOMPANIES?

Record companies need talents of songwriters, entertainers and master producers.

Songwriters may receive income from several sources; the biggest source is the songwriter's share of money paid by record companies to publishers for use of songs on records; the next biggest source is the songwriter's share of money distributed by performance rights societies based on airplay of records containing songs.

Entertainers may receive income from several sources; the biggest source is from personal appearances; the record company does pay money to musicians, background vocalists, artists for performing at sessions, and also pays royalties in large amounts to relatively few recording artists.

Master producers include salaried (and possibly royalty promised) employees of record companies and independent producers. Producers collect money from record companies
    (1)   for selling masters
    (2)   for entering into long-term contracts
    (3)   for selling to record companies existing long-term contracts between the producers and artists
    (4)   for producing masters
    (5)   as royalties.

Record companies pay money to publishers for the use of songs; it is contractually customary for publishers to pay half of that gross income to songwriters. Publishers also receive money based on airplay from performance rights societies. It is very easy to start and administer a small publishing company. Therefore, many (1) songwriters, (2) entertainers, (3) master producers, (4) record companies, (5) others, own publishing companies and fight for the right to publish songs to be recorded.

Many recording artists are also songwriters. Recording artists may also have the talent and bargaining power to produce records featuring themselves.

Thus, the same person may receive royalties as (1) song-writer, (2) publisher, (3) recording artist, (4) master producer.

If he has the abilities, a person may make money as (5) arranger, (6) copyist, (7) musical, (8) background vocalist, (9) engineer.

An entertainer who has many abilities may use one or more abilities in connection with one project, and use other abilities in connection with other projects.

For example, members of a trio may (1) tour for the U.S.O. or on college circuits while building their names and waiting for records featuring them to be released, (2) write songs both for themselves and for other groups, (3) perform as recording artists to produce singles and LPs, (4) perform singly (to avoid furnishing the group sound) as anonymous background vocalists on records featuring other artists. THEN, after a record is or looks as if it might become a big hit, the group may try to tour in places where their box office attractiveness is important.

Your approach to the money record companies pay out directly and indirectly can be divided into:
    (a)   approaching the record companies personnel in charge of acquiring (i) songs, (ii) masters, (iii) artists.
    (b)   approaching publishers
    (c)   approaching independent producers.

Lists of record companies, publishers, master producers are contained in annuals published by Billboard, Cash Box, Record World, in telephone directories, in other trade and fan publications.

Recording studios are located in many places outside New York, Los Angeles, Nashville (in each case there are studios not only in, but near the named cities). Most studios are involved in producing masters and publishing; some studios are involved in additional record company activities.

The biggest record companies are located in the New York

and Los Angeles area. Some of these companies have branch offices in other communities. The companies have business contacts all over the United States.

Persons employed by record companies to discover new talent are pressed for time, and do not have enough time to see everyone who wants to see them.

Record company personnel, in order to best utilize their time, tend to limit their time to dealing with professionals who have achieved track records (who have contributed to hits in the past, preferably the recent past).

Record companies also realize that many hits on the charts feature new artists, who have not had previous hits.

The varieties of mixing the new artists with persons with track records include:
1.   New artists include members of the group who have been a part of other successful artist groups.
2.   New artists include a hot songwriter, who is also writing songs for the new artists.
3.   Other persons concerned with the production (songwriter, arranger, producer) have track records.
4.   New artists have developed tremendous personal appearance following, and/or favorable press notices.

To earn money from record companies, approach record companies.

CHAPTER 22

HOW DO EMPLOYERS RATE ENTERTAINERS?

1. Cooperation and attitude
2. Showmanship
3. Professionalism
4. Audience reaction
5. Drawing power
6. Music accompaniment
7. Arrival
8. Performance start
9. Performance length
10. Music backup
11. Equipment required
12. Contract issued date
13. Executed contract received
14. Agent cooperation
15. Publicity support
16. Personal manager cooperation
17. Road personnel cooperation
18. Price
19. Contract date
20. Contract time — rehearsal
21. Contract time — performance
22. Comments:
    An excellent show
    Very cooperative
    Good rapport with audience
    Astounding musical versatility
    An impressive performance
    Refreshing rock act
    One of the best acts ever
    A superb performance by some true professionals
23. Box office drawing power

CHAPTER 23

HOW YOU CAN HIT IT BIG IN THE
MULTI-BILLION DOLLAR RECORD INDUSTRY !?!

Let's see how others hit it big in the record industry.

Some people started record companies. Herb Alpert and Jerry Moss started A&M Records. Al Bennett and others started Liberty Records, and sold their shares for high amounts of cash and/or stock. Berry Gordy started Motown. Randy Woods started Dot Records, and sold it for millions. Frank Sinatra started Reprise Records, and profitably merged it with Warner Brothers Records. Only a handful of people started Capitol Records.

Some people started publishing companies, and sold them for hundreds of thousands of dollars (or millions of dollars). Others retained their publishing companies and receive royalties.

Songwriters who write all or most songs of many hit albums have made hundreds of thousands of dollars per year — while they were hot.

Entertainers such as The Beatles, Bob Dylan, Elvis Presley, and The Rolling Stones have made millions of dollars, as have several dozen other artists. Relatively few artists consistently fill stadiums; many more artists can fill stadiums while their records are at the top.

Managers often make more money (net) than the artists they manage. An artist who has a gross income of two million dollars, may pay his manager a 25% commission of $500,000, may reimburse his manager's traveling and other expenses of $100,000. The artist may spend the rest of his income on traveling expenses, band, etc., while the manager need spend almost no money for business expenses.

Promoters of live shows risk money on entertainers, advertising, hall, etc. IF the promoter is lucky, he can double and triple his weekly gamble; if he is unlucky he can lose his shirt. Some events and shows have had box office takes of millions of dollars.

Some recording musicians earn over $100,000 per year, mostly working at union scale or double union scale. Some pick up additional money as producers and as artists.

Some master producers have made millions of dollars (sometimes from just one LP). While successful artists may record one or two LPs a year, successful producers may record a dozen or more LPs annually.

Thus, both entrepreneurs and talented people have hit it big in the record industry.

The key lies in getting LOTS OF PEOPLE to do something.

The concert promoter needs LOTS OF PEOPLE attending his concert.

The performer needs LOTS OF PEOPLE willing to attend his concerts and buy his records.

The royalty recipients need LOTS OF PEOPLE buying their records.

CLUE: Your chances to make it big are better if you tie in with big people and companies, than if you don't. (Danger — you may be lost in a big company.)

The big companies have tremendous overhead and have tremendous expenses. Some companies pay their recording artists monthly advances to enable the artists to keep their organizations intact.

You, who are reading this book, MAY make it big in the record industry.

Or, you may not.

Compare yourself with others of your level.

Most others just dream about success, but don't bother preparing themselves.

Most others give up after being rejected. You know enough about the reasons people may turn you down to know that you should go on to find the people who won't turn you down.

Or,possibly, you may be right in giving up.

Lots of people spend their youth in the record industry, and then move into other fields. Possibly they did the right thing in (a) trying and (b) giving up.

The record industry is an industry with extremes and without security. The risks which are challenging adventures to kids, may become burdensome worries to older people.

The steps to making it big include:
    (a)   Improve yourself.
    (b)   Prepare yourself in several fields, so that you can fit in where a talent you possess is needed.
    (c)   Find your team consisting of talented, cooperative and likeable people who are willing to follow you.
    (d)   Be ready to perform when the opportunity comes. (No excuses for missing members, transportation, equipment.)
    (e)   Read this book and the other books on the industry. (Business and law books, in addition to fan and buff books.)
    (f)   Get in touch with the big people, who are big enough to help you.
    (g)   Analyze who spends money in your area, what you could do to have that person spend money on you. For example, who could and would consider every cent spent to build you and your group as valuable advertising for his product or store.
    (h)   Present to the person whose help you want:
        — that your talent can make money for him.
        — that you are likeable, loyal, reliable.

Many people destroy themselves by being unreliable, or

playing games which make them appear unreliable.

With thousands of newcomers every year trying to compete with you to become big in the record industry, you may find the going rough.

But, year after year, some people have made it big.

Maybe, you will, too.

Or, maybe you won't. You can bet on one thing — most of your competitors won't.

Hope you will enjoy whatever you do.

Look at this picture — if each year over 15,000 singles and over 15,000 LPs are released, then there is a tremendous demand at recording level for new songs and new artists. If over $2 billion worth of records and tapes are sold annually there is a tremendous demand at customer level for new and old songs and artists.

If you can collect for yourself a mere 1% of the retail dollar, you would be collecting $20,000,000.00.

CHAPTER 24

INCOME TAXES

The United States and most individual states have laws concerning income taxes.

Taxpayers are supposed to keep track of their income, their expenses, compute net taxable income, pay any estimated and any annual taxes which may be due.

Many entertainers are paid as independent contractors (full fees with no deductions); other entertainers are paid as employees (gross salary, less U.S. income tax withheld, less state income tax withheld, less social security withheld, less state unemployment insurance or disability insurance withheld).

Entertainers often are "small businesses." This includes the 16 year old leader of a trio playing for pay at dances; the songwriter who creates, handles the paperwork, and tries to persuade potential song users to use the songwriter's songs.

Other entertainers may be "partners." This may include the three members of a trio, which trio receives income, pays expenses, splits the rest. A songwriter and her mother may be partners, the songwriter providing the talent and time, the mother providing the capital (house, telephone, transportaion, money), with the parties intending to split any profit.

The Internal Revenue Service provides free pamphlets, and sells some inexpensive booklets which are revised annually TAX GUIDE FOR SMALL BUSINESS, etc.

Many show businesses are profitable; many are unprofitable. Especially in early years when many entertainers are still given monetary gifts by parents, entertainers' business expenses may exceed their business income. Because unemployment insurance payments to an entertainer are not included in gross income for tax reasons, but the business expenses paid for are deductible, a maturer entertainer may operate his business at a loss. There are various advantages to an entertainer if he files tax returns showing true losses.

Many of expenses are ORDINARY and NECESSARY business expenses, and are deduct ible on tax returns. Be sure to keep proof that you incurred the expenses, so that in the event your tax return is audited, you can substantiate your deductible expenses.

CHAPTER 25

INTERDEPENDENCE

Do you have a perception of the inescapable interdependence of each segment of the record industry upon each other?

The artist and the record company need each other to record masters. The artist needs record company promotion to achieve initial airplay. The record company may or may not need the artist's live appearance to generate a following to generate sales.

The promoter needs record company induced radio airplay to make the artist hot in the area at the time of the personal appearance. The promoter needs radio commercials to advertise events.

Radio needs records for inexpensive programming and radio needs money for commercials from record companies and public appearance locations.

The entertainer may visit radio stations in person, by telephone, by pre-recorded tape containing praises for local announcers to read their scripted portions. The radio station has interesting free programming, the entertainer obtains publicity for himself, the record company and the promoter.

Trade and fan magazines educate the readers in news, editorial, and advertising pages; the magazines publicize entertainers, record companies, concerts, etc.; the magazines obtain money for advertisements from record companies.

CHAPTER 26

THE LEAD SHEET

Many songwriters are illiterate, in that they don't know
how to read or to write music. These songwriters may use a
specialized LEAD SHEET service to set forth the song on
paper. Many songwriters have taken the time and trouble to
become literate, and write their own lead sheets. LEAD
SHEET services may charge anywhere from $5 to $40 per song,
depending on the amount of work they do (prepare rough
pencil draft only; prepare inked onion skin; prepare ozalid or
other photocopies), the length of the song (a 2 minute song
generally requires 2 or 3 pages), professional standing (a
college music student may charge less, an established business
servicing professionals may charge more, a mail order business
servicing amateurs often charges even more).

CHAPTER 27

LYRICIST AND THE COMPOSER /
ALTERNATE PROVISIONS IN THEIR CONTRACT

Re: I AM LOVEABLE, I AM GREAT, I AM HERE.

1. *Larry Lyricist* Has written lyrics and owns all rights in them. If and when the rights in the lyrics are assigned to a publisher, such contract shall provide that *Larry Lyricist* shall receive the lyricist's portion of royalties only.

2. For example, if the publisher grants a mechanical license to use the song to a record company, and only the melody is used, then all of the songwriter's share of royalties received from such record company shall belong to *Carol Composer.*

3. For example, if a French translation is made by a lyricist writing in French, then *Larry Lyricist* and the French lyricist shall share the lyricist's half of the songwriter's share of royalties, while *Carol Composer* shall receive the entire composer's half of the songwriters share of royalties.

This chapter has introduced several concepts: Among them are:
1. two persons may share income in various proportions;
2. the creator who has more business and legal knowledge can take monetary advantage over his co-creator with less business and legal knowledge,
3. knowledge is required concerning foreign uses of songs and masters.

CHAPTER 28

LYRICS

Lyrics (the words of a song) are written by a lyricist.

Larry Lyricist wrote:
> Sound the Guitars and the Drums
> For at last I have come
> I am Loveable,
> I am Great,
> I am Here.

The creator of lyrics of a song has, by law, a common law *copyright* in his lyrics. Nobody has the *right to copy* the lyrics, except the owner of the common law copyright and people who are given permission to copy the lyrics by the owner of the common law copyright.

The lyricist has created and owns the lyrics of a potential song. A song may have lyrics and music; sometimes a song only has music. Sometimes lyrics (without music) are called a poem or a song poem.

CHAPTER 29

MANAGER – GROUP RELATIONS

The manager frequently is able to SELL HIS GROUP to others – to promoters of concerts and dances, to night clubs and bowling alleys with live entertainment, to producers of records and television shows.

Frequently the customer of the group's services buys the group's services because they buy the manager. They believe him when he says the group can draw, can perform, and that all of the group (with all of its equipment in working order) will appear on time all the time.

But the manager frequently commits an oversight – he forgets that he must keep selling himself to the members of his group. He must sell his past, his present, his future.

Do the members of the group know and think about the past activities of the manager?

It was (or was it) the manager who helped four (or five, six, seven, etc.) individuals who played instruments and/or sang and/or looked great to create out of a mixture that miracle which is a commercial group.

It was the manager who helped keep the group together with encouragement, providing rehearsal facilities, "kicking ass" to get semi-responsible, musically talented, immature, youngsters to attend to the business of coming on time to rehearsals, auditions, night club jobs, recording sessions, planning sessions, photography and other publicity sessions, etc.

It was the manager who found the people who paid money for the group for playing and for performing.

It was the manager who checked out job offers by checking out the reputation of the potential employer, checking out the locale and location, checking out the sound and light and stage facilities.

But does the group know enough about the past to realize how much they benefited from the services of the manager?

Let's go to the present. Does the group know how much the manager did for the group on the day the group played at a big dance?

The probable answer is "NO."

1. The group did not have money to pay the entire motel bill. The motel refused to let the group take out its equipment. The group called the manager, at his office. The manager drove to the motel and advanced his money to pay the motel bill.

2. The group's van's motor failed to work properly. The manager called a car and truck rental company and used his credit to obtain a van.

3. The group and the manager — in the past — had discussed whether the group would carry its own instruments or whether assistant equipment managers would be employed. (They had agreed that one equipment repairman would be with the group all the time and that his title would be "equipment manager").

4. They had discussed the possible functions of assistant equipment managers: securing girls, securing drugs, transporting equipment, carrying equipment, setting up equipment on stage, GUARDING THE EQUIPMENT, relieving musicians from the physically tiring problem of carrying heavy and bulky equipment before show time and after show time, GOPHER functions (go for coffee, go for cheeseburgers, go for trade papers).

CHAPTER 30

MANY TAXES

1. YOU PAY
When you receive money
U.S. income tax
State income tax
Collect + pay over State sales tax
City license fee based in part on gross receipts.

2. YOU PAY
When you employ someone
Employer pays: U.S.F.U.T.A. (Federal
Unemployment Tax Act)
Employer pays: State U.I. (Unemployment
Insurance)
Employer pays: U.S.F.I.C.A. (also known as
Social Security)
Employer withholds: U.S.F.I.C.A.
Employer withholds: U.S. income tax
Employer withholds: State income tax
Employer withholds: State D.I. (Disability
Insurance)

NOTE: In some states, the employee pays Unemployment
Insurance. In some states, the employer pays Disability Insurance.
Tax laws differ in various states.

3. YOU PAY
When you buy something
Sales taxes

4. YOU PAY
When you own something
Real property taxes
Personal property taxes
Car license fees

5. YOU PAY
When you give or leave something to others
Gift Tax — U.S. and State   Estate Tax — U.S.
Inheritance Tax or Estate Tax — State

6. YOU MAY PAY

Penalty for paying late
Penalty for filing late
Interest for paying late
Penalty for negligence
Penalty for fraud
Penalty if you are supposed to pay somebody else's
taxes and you did not (SPECIAL STATUTES).

CHAPTER 31

MASTER PRODUCING COMPANIES

If we may distinguish between (1) sound track production and (2) distribution of records, then we are ready for the next step: Many companies produce sound tracks and then sell their rights in the sound tracks to other companies which finance and distribute records.

The production of phonograph record masters (soundtracks) may vary in cost from almost $0 (the musicians are paid nothing, the recording studio supplies its facilities in exchange for publishing, tape must be paid for) to over $100,000 for 30 minutes of usable music.

A master producer selects the musical compositions, hires the arranger, musicians, and vocalists, rents the recording studio, personally or has an assistant "produce" (direct) the recording session and mix the tracks. The master producer may do this on speculation in the hope he can persuade a record company to sign a long term recording contract covering the recording of the artist in the future, or the producer may be performing his functions pursuant to the provisions of an existing contract with a record company.

Producers may make money:
1. Receiving a flat fee for recording an artist (or commercial).
2. Receiving royalties on masters he produces.
3. Receiving front money selling his rights in a master to a record company.
4. Releasing an artist from a contract.
5. As a songwriter.
6. As a publisher.
7. As a manager.
8. Receiving kickbacks from a recording studio selected by the producer and paid by a record company. (FRAUD)
9. Receiving kickbacks from musicians paid union scale by the record company at the behest of the producer. (CRIME)

CHAPTER 32

MECHANICAL LICENSE ROYALTY DUE DATES

	1.	2.	3.	4.	5.
Name of Song					
Date of License					
Record Co. Name & Address					
Record No. & Artist					
Annual Royalty Due Dates					
Royalties Recd. Dates					
Amount Royalties Recd.					
Date Song-writers Paid					

CHAPTER 33

MUSIC

Music is written by a composer. Frequently the same person writes both the lyrics and the music of a song. Sometimes two people will work together; each will contribute some of the lyrics and some of the music. Sometimes, one co-writer will contribute the music, while another co-writer writes the music.

Carol Composer wrote a melody in her mind, sang the melody out loud, played it on her piano, then played it on her guitar.

CHAPTER 34

MUSIC EDUCATORS

Many music educators are members of such organizations as Music Educators National Conference, American Choral Directors Association, American String Teachers Association, College Band Directors National Association, National Association of College Wind and Percussion Instructors, National Association of Jazz Educators, National Band Association, National School Orchestra Association, Florida Music Educators Association, Florida Bandmasters Association, Florida College Music Educators Association, Florida Elementary Music Educators Association, Florida Orchestra Association, Florida Vocal Association, Florida Association of Jazz Educators, etc.

If you belong to these or any other musical or non-musical associations, analyze each to see whether they can help you as an institution or as individuals, by

(1) financing recording, pressing, printing, advertising,
(2) buying records,
(3) publicizing the records with stories or advertisements in MUSIC EDUCATORS JOURNAL, FLORIDA MUSIC DIRECTOR, and/or other publications.

Many professional entertainers, who receive no or almost no money from their recording activities, are content because these activities create records which publicize the artist and enhance his career as a live performer.

Many teachers, who receive no or almost no money from their recording activities, are content because these activities create records which publicize the teacher and enhance his career as a live performer.

CHAPTER 35

THE MUSIC PUBLISHER

The music publisher is in the business of:

(a)   acquiring songs (rights in songs).

(b)   merchandising the songs (preparing lead sheets, demonstration records and tapes when desirable).

(c)   performing paperwork (contracts with the songwriter, the record companies; sending forms to the Copyright Office and the performing rights society).

(d)   promoting the song (persuading persons selecting music for recording, television or other purposes to use the music) and records using the song (persuading radio stations to play and newspapers/magazines to publicize records containing the song).

(e)   collecting money from users of the song, from the performance rights society, from foreign sub-publishers.

(f)   paying the appropriate amounts to the songwriter(s).

(g)   etc.

CHAPTER 36

MUSIC RETAILER

Different stores which sell records have different motives.

RECORD STORE: Kids come in to buy best selling hits. Once they are in the store, they buy more singles and albums.

RECORD — MUSIC HARDWARE STORE: We lay out our store so that customers who come in for records must walk through the TV — Tape Recorder — Radio — Phonograph sections. That way, when our record customers want a high priced item, they will habitually come to us.

DEPARTMENT STORE: The way to bring in teenagers and get them into the habit of buying all kinds of merchandise in the department store, is to give big discounts on records.

CHAPTER 37

MUSIC RETAIL STORES

We strongly recommend that entertainers and future entertainers try to work in stores selling records. First of all, such work is one way of making peanuts and buying instruments at discounts. More important, such work should provide excellent experience which the entertainer can use later to prod his record company into cooperating with retailers. Thirdly, entertainers looking for ways of staying at home and in show business may feel more at home in distribution and retailing if they had such business experience as a youngster.

For insights into music retailing, we recommend MUSIC RETAILER, Larkin Publications, Inc., 50 Hunt Street, Watertown, Massachusetts 02172.
(Possibly subscriptions will not have climbed from $6.00 per year, $10.00 for 2 years.)

CHAPTER 38

NATIONAL EDUCATIONAL CONFERENCE

The National Education Conference states about itself "NEC is an organization of college and university program staffs that was founded to enable students and faculty on various campuses to share information about programming, establish training programs and arrange cooperative programming."

The NEC Newsletter is published eight times a year for the members and associate members of the National Entertainment Conference. P.O. Box 11489 – Capitol Station, Columbia, South Carolina 29211.

Full membership ($75 per fiscal year, $10 of which is for the NEC Newsletter) is restricted to institutions of higher education; associate membership is restricted to firms whose products or services are directly related to the field of college entertainment.

Since knowing more about potential employers and their policies seems a good way for an artist to obtain jobs and satisfy customers, it appears worthwhile for entertainers and their representatives to read each issue of the NEC Newsletter and to learn whatever NEC cares to teach in conferences, etc.

Promoters and entertainers find NEC Newsletter checklists and articles very useful.

CHAPTER 39

NATIONAL MUSIC PUBLISHERS' ASSOCIATION

In the May 14, 1917 issue of *Variety,* a full-page advertisement appeared officially announcing the organization of the Music Publishers' Protective Association, the name by which the organization was to be known until 1966, when it was changed to the National Music Publishers' Association (NMPA).

The ad stated in part: "The general objectives of the Association shall be to maintain high standards of commercial honor and integrity among its members; to promote and inculcate just and equitable principles of trade and business, and to foster and encourage the art of music and song writing."

The necessity of such an organization had become increasingly apparent.

In the 1880's and 1890's, a new popular music publishing business had emerged with the rise of a great demand for sheet music to be played on the piano, which, itself, had recently become a fashionable fixture in middle-class homes. This event coincided with the development of better transportation and, thus, more convenient travel for the performers who popularized new songs. A new breed of music publisher had become a dynamic force in the business — the publisher who, for the first time, comprehended that songs could be popularized by consistent and persistent repetition . . . by plugging.

By 1917, when the association was founded, vaudeville was king, and it was the main medium through which songs were popularized by youthful and progressive publishers. It was in this historical framework that the Association came into being. The objectives as stated in advertisements were promoted and pursued.

The Association focused on other broad activities as well and increasingly undertook the two common objectives of all trade associations (which were becoming more and more a factor in American business); (1) to protect and (2) to advance the interests of their industries.

All trade associations differ, depending upon the nature of the product or service involved. However, the publishing business is unique in that its existence is fundamentally based on a law — the copyright law. Indeed, it was the passage of the new Copyright Law of 1909 which stimulated the growth of the music publishing business by modernizing the law and establishing new rights. The property on which the industry is based is created by authors and composers, but the protection of this intellectual property — copyright — is defined by law and its scope is limited by law. Policy and philosophical considerations of copyright are complex and cannot be dealt with here, nor can the moral aspects of authorship which are inherent in this peculiar type of property. Let it suffice to say that music publishing — as most other areas of publishing — can exist only by virtue of the copyright law and the public's respect thereof, and that copyright in music, because of the great variety of means by which it is communicated, is, of all areas of copyright, the most complex.

To describe the history and achievements of NMPA, we should, therefore, start with that characteristic which makes it unique from other trade associations.

MUSIC PUBLISHING IS A COPYRIGHT INDUSTRY

The copyright statute which prevails at this time was passed in 1909, only eight years before the establishment of NMPA. It was an undoubted improvement over the Law of 1870, concerning which President Theodore Roosevelt wrote in a message to Congress:

They are imperfect in definition, confused and inconsistent in expression; they omit provision for many articles which, under modern reproductive processes are entitled to protection; they impose hardship upon the copyright proprietor which are not essential to the fair protection of the public; they are difficult for the courts to interpret and impossible for the Copyright Office to administer with satisfaction to the public. Attempts to improve them by amendment have been frequent, no less than twelve acts having been passed since the revised statute. To perfect them by further amendment seems impractical. A complete revision of them is essential.

While the new law of 1909 was designed to accomplish the purposes set down by President Roosevelt, nevertheless there is often a considerable difference between the intent of legislators in drafting a law and the manner in which it works in practice. Moreover, in the more than six decades since 1909, technological and cultural changes have continued at an accelerating pace.

Thus, one of the major functions of NMPA since its earliest days has been to cope with uncertainities in which the law may seem less than clear, to seek interpretation of the law as new developments and uses have created problems not contemplated in 1909, and to deal with the practicalities of the administration of copyrights.

Copyright Lawmaking in Legislation

It wasn't long after the passage of the copyright statute in 1909 that certain flaws became apparent, and as early as 1924, efforts were made to revise it. These efforts for revision either in general or in regard to special provisions have continued through the years and, in all of them, NMPA was obviously concerned and active on behalf of music publishers. The specific provision of the law which most concerns music publishers and The Harry Fox Agency relates to the recording rate. Under the 1909 law, once a copyright proprietor has granted permission to anyone for the commercial recording of a work, others may also make recordings of that work by following certain simple procedures provided by law. The original purpose of this provision — the compulsory license — was to guard against the creation of a monopoly by one record caompny which might be able to tie up the exclusive right to record substantial numbers of musical works and deprive its competitors of access to them. The statutory royalty for the recording of a composition was established under a compulsory license at 2¢ a copy in 1909. This rate continues in effect today!

The first step for a comprehensive revision of the U.S. copyright laws took place in the mid-1950's. Representatives of NMPA were included in the panel of experts which debated the issues and which was instrumental in the drafting of a revision bill introduced in Congress in 1964. NMPA's position concerning the compulsory licensing of recordings had been simple — that it be eliminated. However, through a series of compromises, publishers unwillingly acquiesced to its continuation provided that there was an increase in the statutory royalty which would establish a reasonable contemporary and continuing ceiling under which the copyright proprietor and record manufacturers could negotiate. At this writing, the conflict over the statutory royalty between the recording industry and the music publishing industry continues, with NMPA urging that only a reasonable percentage royalty can provide authors and their publishers, the recording industry, and the public with a basis which would have sufficient flexibility to adapt itself to change in the economy and the industry. It is hoped this conflict will be resolved satisfactorily and fairly when Congress finally passes the Copyright Revision bill, which at this time is still awaiting enactment.

The preoccupation with this specific issue should not suggest that NMPA lacks interest in all areas of copyright revision. Through these many long years of its involvement in the legislative process, its staff and Washington representatives have worked diligently toward a law which protects fundamental rights and interests of writers and publishers in all fields.

During the period of consideration of copyright revision and in anticipation of its enactment, NMPA has been among those who have worked and achieved extension of subsisting copyrights which would otherwise expire, so that the writers or their heirs would not be deprived of the benefits of the longer term of copyright as provided in the Bill. These efforts have, thus far, been successful.

Infringements of copyrights — whether for profit or convenience — have been a concern of the Association from its earliest days. A major step toward improving the law in this area was achieved in 1971, when, together with the recording industry, NMPA successfully urged the passage of a law which, for the first time, made unauthorized duplication of records and tapes illegal. This law also includes a section of great importance to music publishers. Previously, the copyright law had provided only treble damages as a penalty for infringing music copyrights in recordings. For the first time the full scope of remedies became available in this field — $250 minimum statuatory damages, criminal penalties, etc.

As a matter of policy and practice, NMPA has continued to be involved constructively in all legislative matters which touch upon copyright directly or indirectly.

Copyright in Practice —
The Harry Fox Agency

In the world of music, there are hundreds of thousands of copyrights and tens of thousands of users who seek access to them. Manifestly, it would be economically prohibitive for hundreds of individual copyright proprietors to negotiate licenses with and monitor their rights to royalties from hundreds of individual users. It has been essential, therefore, to create organizations which simplify the clearance of rights and the development of a functioning marketplace.

In 1914, the American Society of Composers, Authors and Publishers (ASCAP) was established for the purpose of licensing musical copyrights for public performance. Needless to say, music publishers played a dynamic role in the creation and development of this new apparatus. However, ASCAP and, since 1940, Broadcast Music, Inc. (BMI) are responsible only for licensing of performance. In 1927, when motion pictures first talked and sang, there was considerable confusion over the acquisition of licenses by producers to synchronize copyrighted music with their movies.

NMPA recognized the practical necessity of creating an efficient vehicle which producers could employ in seeking rights for music and which music publishers could utilize in licensing these rights. E. Claude Mills, then Chairman of the Board of NMPA, was appointed to carry out this service, which was made available to all publishers, whether or not they were members of the Association, as all services of The Harry Fox Agency are today. The licensing service proved to be of great value to all concerned, and in 1936 it was extended to include the licensing of electrical transcriptions under the direction of Mr. Mills' successor, John G. Paine.

During its early years, NMPA was concerned with problems regarding phonograph recordings and piano rolls. As early as 1922, there were discussions about the necessity of auditing certain record companies; in fact, audits were undertaken. On several occasions, licensing forms were prepared and recommended for use by the industry. However, it was only in 1938 that licensing of recordings and collection of mechanical royalties and their distribution was undertaken by the new agent, Harry Fox.

As the trade association of the popular music publishing industry, NMPA developed a licensing service which today collects on behalf of its clients in excess of $45,000,000 annually and is one of the largest organizations of its kind in the world, serving over 3,500 publishers in the field of recordings. For its services in issuing mechanical licenses, collecting royalties and distributing them to publishers, as well as for the periodic audits of record manufacturers, The Harry Fox Agency presently charges a basic fee of 3½%, which is the lowest fee charged by any of the mechanical licensing organizations which have been established in most countries of the world as a result of the economic necessity of using common licensing organizations. In part, this low fee is an indication of the efficiency and effectiveness of its operation.

The Harry Fox Agency maintains continuing liaison with mechanical licensing organizations throughout the world, with particular emphasis on the safeguarding of American copyrights which are not represented by subpublishers in various countries. Studies of mechanical licensing and collection in Latin America have been undertaken, and, increasingly, the expertise of the organization has been sought by mechanical licensing organizations in process of establishment or in a developing state to assist them in their progress toward effective operation.

In 1969, when Harry Fox died, Albert Berman — his long-time associate — was appointed Managing Director of The Harry Fox Agency, which was then incorporated as a wholly owned subsidiary of NMPA. Additional information about the Harry Fox Agency will be found in later pages.

Two unrelated problems involved in copyright have led NMPA and The Harry Fox Agency on behalf of individual publishers to seek relief before the courts on an almost continuing basis. The first — and most interesting — has been the desirability of seeking interpretation of the copyright law through litigation, either because the law itself was unclear in its language or intent OR because changing uses of music had created new questions as to the application of the law in areas which had not been forseen in 1909. As a result, the Association and The Harry Fox Agency have been involved in many, many lawsuits over the years on behalf of individual publisher plaintiffs and as *amicus curiae.* Listing the important actions and decisions would require more space than is available here. Indeed, our victories are well-known among members of the copyright bar.

The Association and The Harry Fox Agency have spent even more time in the courts in order to cope with their second problem: actions against those who infringe on the rights granted copyright proprietors under the statute.

Piracy has been rife since the beginnings of printing and has been an ever-present problem of the Association since its establishment. A primary concern has been the unauthorized duplication of printed product. It has always been the policy of NMPA to help protect the copyrights of its members. In the early 1920's, attempts were made to develop a paper which would thwart those who counterfeited sheet music. In the 1930's, song sheets containing lyrics of standard songs and current hits began to appear in alarming numbers. This occurrence menaced sheet music sales, then the main source of publishers' income, and the Association, on behalf of individual publishers, frequently instituted investigative and legal action in cooperation with law enforcement agencies. By the diligence of music publishers' efforts in courts, illegal song sheets disappeared from the market. Once again, in the 1960's, it was necessary to take similar action against fake books — large collections containing hundreds of lead sheets of familiar songs sold at relatively low prices. This infringement of copyright has been — if not eliminated — driven underground.

Today the development of photo-duplication presents a new threat, and the Association is prepared to cope with a new type of infringement which, more often than not, is undertaken for convenience rather than for profit, but which deprives writers and publishers of their legitimate markets.

Both NMPA and The Harry Fox Agency, on behalf of individual publishers (members and clients), have been active in continuing efforts through invocations of the legal process to hold for copyright infringement unauthorized duplicators of recordings and tapes as well as printed music.

A Copyright Industry Internationally

Although the United States was not a member of any International Copyright Convention until 1955, international relations have been an important factor throughout the Association's history. The preeminence of the American song throughout the world and the impact of our native musical developments created an international market for American copyrights over a half-century ago. International copyright was secured through the so-called back door of the Berne Convention by simultaneous publication in a country which was a Berne member. When the Universal Copyright Convention (UCC) was drafted as an international instrument specifically designed in consideration of the pecularities of American copyright law, NMPA was among the active proponents of ratification by the United States, which was accomplished in 1954.

Since then, NMPA has played an even more active role. For the first time at the Berne Convention Revision Conference in Stockholm in 1967, a representative of American music publishing interests was included in an American delegation of observers. Subsequently, the Association was, and continues to be, represented on the U.S. State Department Panel of Advisors on International Copyright. NMPA was a member of the United States Delegation to Berne and UCC Revision Conferences which took place in Paris in 1971. A specific exemption of the lyrics of musical works from the compulsory license provisions for translations was achieved at this meeting after the idea was proposed and pursued by NMPA's representative. The long-range implications of this may prove to be of considerable future importance. Most recently, an NMPA representative was a member of the U.S. Delegation to the Diplomatic Conference in Geneva, where an International Convention against the unauthorized duplication of recordings was drafted and adapted.

In other facets of international relations, both NMPA and The Harry Fox Agency have been increasingly active. In April, 1973, NMPA was elected an Associate Member of The International Confederation of Societies of Authors and Composers (CISAC). The Association was greatly honored to join with the more than fifty members dedicated "to insuring the safeguarding, respect and protection of the moral and professional interests attaching to every kind of literary and artistic property and to watch over and contribute to the respecting of economic and legal interests attaching to the said productions both in the international sphere and that of national legislation."

As a member of the music section of the International Publishers' Association (IPA), an NMPA member served as a vice president, and NMPA has been active in deliberations and decisions of that organization.

Among other services provided by NMPA to its members is a continuing flow of information on new foreign copyright laws, as well as the necessary procedures to assure copyright where special circumstances have prevailed.

NMPA AS A TRADE ASSOCIATION

The general activities of NMPA — other than its unique character as the association of a copyright industry — can be grouped into four general categories.

Government Relations

The role of government, whether through legislation or through the regulatory powers of federal departments and bureaus, has had an increasing impact on every business. NMPA constantly follows government activities, takes action when necessary, and, on occasion, has initiated legislation specifically in the interests of the music publishing industry.

To list all of NMPA's activities vis-a-vis the federal government over a period of more than fifty years is not possible here. We therefore cite only those of special importance, together with some others which may serve to indicate the scope of this facet of our trade association work.

A special tax exception for the music publishing business was introduced at NMPA's initiative in Congress in the 1950's and was enacted into law. The personal holding provisions of the tax law had created a considerable hardship for many members of the industry and — if they had not been corrected by an amendment to the tax laws — would have imposed an increasing handicap on their financial operations.

The preferential educational postal rates were extended to include all music through joint action of the Association with other interested groups.

In the international field, NMPA was among those organizations which specifically pressed for United States ratification of the Florence Agreement and enactment of the enabling legislation which made this country a party to the treaty which eliminates tariffs on educational and cultural materials.

Also on the international scene, a special study has been undertaken on the tax structure in various countries as it affects the earnings of United States copyrights abroad. Possible courses of action are being explored by NMPA and others to improve the situation.

Appropriations by the federal government for programs which are of interest to music — whether the programs be in education, the arts, or another field — have been a matter of continuing interest and support.

Not only is positive action necessary to advance the interests of music publishers, but also it has frequently been necessary to safeguard the industry's well-being by opposing detrimental proposals. This has been done wherever necessary.

During both World Wars, NMPA was the force which mobilized the industry in the spirit of the war effort and worked with the government in framing workable controls during these emergency periods. The same role was assumed during the Depression, when regulations were similarly in effect.

It is not only on the national scene that NMPA has been involved with government matters. From time to time, legislation, which has been supported — or opposed — by the Association, has been introduced in the various states. However, it must be admitted that constant scrutiny in each state is impossible practically for any but the largest trade associations.

Information

NMPA serves as an information center in two ways: to the industry and to the public.

In the realm of statistics, it is interesting to note that most inquiries develop outside of the industry. Since figures are becoming of increasing importance, greater emphasis has been placed on their accumulation and availability. For example, the first comprehensive study of the total volume and sale of printed music was undertaken in 1973 and, based on a determination of its usefulness, far more specialized surveys may be made in the future.

More important to our members, however, is the study of technological developments and their evaluation in terms of potential impact. The history of NMPA is obviously the history of almost six decades of American popular music, and that history is largely a consequence of the manner in which the communication of music has changed. As long ago as 1922, the Association was examining the problems and potential of commercial radio as it came into being. The consequences of talking pictures have already been noted as they led to licensing functions. The advent of the long-playing record also required study as to its implications. Most recently, video cassettes, cable television, and satellites have been the subjects of a comprehensive symposium and report.

There are a number of special informational services performed by the Association for its industry. Special Reports are prepared on various matters of immediate interest. Among them have been — in the recent past — video cassettes; new copyright laws of various countries; new significant international copyright developments; and interpretations of government activities which affect music publishing, such as the wage and price freezes. At least once a year, a symposium or seminar is held dealing with a subject of primary interest.

Public Relations

Public relations is an activity common to all trade associations. At NMPA they are considered a means rather than an end in themselves. Thus, over the years — particularly through the trade papers — the activities of the Association as well as its position and policy on the many issues which have arisen over the years have been fully covered.

The *NMPA Bulletin* is published at least six times a year for members and friends of NMPA. Its circulation is international, and by many it is considered unique in that it presents news and comments covering the wide gamut of matters of concern and interest to music publishers.

Relations with Other Organizations

Over the years, constructive and cordial relations have been maintained with other organizations, both within the music field and outside it.

The licensing of performing rights of music publishers represents a major source of income, and this licensing is exercised by the three performing rights organizations: ASCAP, BMI, and SESAC. NMPA has never been involved in the workings of these three organizations in carrying out their functions. Nevertheless, in such areas as copyright, there is mutual concern and the exchange of points of view.

Songwriters and publishers are in effect partners. A music publisher is an extension of the writer. The author and composer create the song. The publisher's responsibility is to activate the song by securing recordings, performances, and other types of uses; he also secures the copyright and acts to protect it at all times. He prints the music or licenses others to do so, and he promotes the song on a continuing basis whenever possible to achieve continuing recording and performance revenue as well as the sales of various editions. He also arranges for the international representation of the song in foreign countries throughout the world. Domestically and internationally, the publisher administers the copyright.

The partnership between publisher and songwriter came into being in the early days of Tin Pan Alley, and it has given basic and lasting benefits to both of the partners. Because of this songwriter-publisher relationship NMPA has worked closely with the American Guild of Authors and Composers in achieving joint purposes. It is historically true, however, that ever since the development of printing, writers and publishers do have conflicts, and over the years there have been differences of opinion between the two organizations. However, in recent years a greater awareness of common causes has brought songwriters and publishers closer together, and there exists less emphasis on those controversies which separate them.

There are three other music publishers' trade associations: The Music Publishers' Association of the United States, whose members publish educational and concert music; the Church Music Publishers' Association; and The International Gospel Music Publishers' Association. Each specializes, of course, in its own field; but in the areas of protecting rights and in expanding the market for printed music, there is a community of interest.

Despite the sharp conflict between record manufacturers and music publishers on the mechanical royalty rate, NMPA has made common cause with the Recording Industry Association of America in several areas of common concern. This has been true, as well, in the international field with the International Federation of Phonographic Industries.

The American Music Conference is a trade organization

which includes all facets of the music industry. NMPA financially supports the activities of this organization and sits on its Board of Trustees. Financial support is also given to The Copyright Society of the United States, and here, too, an NMPA official is a member of the Board. The National Music Council (NMC), chartered by an act of Congress, is made up of sixty music organizations which represent the entire world of music, totalling over 1,500,000 individual members. NMPA was one of the founders of the Council, and its Executive Vice President is currently NMC's President. National Music Week, which is an activity of the 600,000-member National Federation of Music Clubs, is, in part, underwritten by NMPA.

Other music organizations with which NMPA maintains continuing liaison and involvement are the National Academy of Recording Arts and Sciences, The National Association of Jazz Educators, the Music Educators National Conference, and Young Audiences.

Interests of music publishers and of book publishers are similar and frequently identical. A very close relationship is maintained with their trade association, the Association of American Publishers, in numerous areas.

—— —— —— —— ——

Any report such as this must be, by its very nature, impersonal. Yet, no account of an organization and its activities could be complete without some reference to people — the people responsible for its accomplishments and its achievements.

For almost six decades a succession of leaders of the music publishing industry has served as NMPA officers and directors and devoted themselves conscientiously and unselfishly toward the solution of new and continuing problems. Other industry volunteers have been dedicated committee members. Recognition is also due to the executives of the Association and the Agency and to their staffs.

In sum it is truly people who have made it possible and will make it possible for NMPA to serve the industry.

The Natioanl Music Publishers' Association is a nonprofit corporation organized under the laws of the State of New York. Its bylaws state: "Any person, firm or corporation or partnership actively engaged in the business of publishing music in the United States of America for a period of at least one year, whose musical publications have been used or distributed on a commercial scale or who assumes the financial risk involved in the normal publication of musical works, shall be eligible as a member." Members are elected by a majority vote of the Board of Directors.

The fifteen Directors of the Association are elected by the membership every two years at the Annual Meeting which takes place on the second Tuesday of May each year. The officers are elected by the Board and are members of the industry — with the exception of the Executive Vice President, the chief managerial officer, who is appointed by the Board of Directors.

Special membership meetings are held in Nashville and Los Angeles each year, providing for in-person reports by the management of the Association and The Harry Fox Agency and an opportunity for open discussion, questions, and answers.

Although NMPA owns The Harry Fox Agency, there is no obligation for members to license their mechanical or synchronization rights through that agency. Nor is it necessary for publishers utilizing the services of The Harry Fox Agency to be members of NMPA.

The membership of the Association has, in the last several years, grown rapidly and now represents all facets of the popular music publishing business in the several geographic areas of the country in which there is substantial music publishing activity today.

An application for membership may be obtained upon request.   *Membership in NMPA is an affirmative expression of a music publisher's committment of responsibility to and participation in his industry.*

CHAPTER 40

NEGOTIATING THE PUBLISHING
(The following are just a few of the possibilities)

ENTERTAINER-SONGWRITER-PUBLISHER
I am the songwriter.
I can do simple paperwork.
I can sing my own songs.
I don't want covers on my records.
I want to keep full publishing rights.

RECORD PRODUCER-PUBLISHER
I am a businessman.
My business income comes from record producing and publishing.
I want to have full publishing.

ENTERTAINER-SONGWRITER-PUBLISHER
Let's split publishing. I'll administer the publishing. I'll pay you one-half of the publisher's share of gross receipts. (Publisher's share = gross receipts - songwriter's share.)

RECORD PRODUCER-PUBLISHER
I agree to the idea of splitting publishing. BUT, I want to be the administrative publisher. I will charge 10% of gross receipts for my services. Then I'll deduct the songwriter's share. I'll split the remainder with you.

ENTERTAINER-SONGWRITER-PUBLISHER
I'll keep all of publishing, but I'll give your record company a mechanical license of 1½¢ per record.

RECORD PRODUCER-PUBLISHER
You can keep publishing. Give me a mechanical license of 1¢ a record plus ½ of ASCAP performance fees paid to the publisher.

CHAPTER 41

NEGOTIABLE DEDUCTIONS FROM GROSS ROYALTIES RECORD COMPANY – ARTIST CONTRACT

1. Cash advances to artist.
2. Actual costs of recording artist

   a. arranger   h. AFM EPW
   b. copyist   i. AFM H & W
   c. conductor   j. AFTRA 5% of Scale
   d. sidemen   k. recording studio
   e. background vocalists   l. tape
   f. artists   m. engineer
   g. cartage

3. One-time costs concerning LP and tapes

   a. liner notes
   b. art work
   c. photography
   d. color separation

4. Bookkeeping playthings.

   a. Actual returns of records on which royalties have been paid.
   b. Discounts, credits, imagination, cheating
   c. Reserves for returns
   d. Kicks.

CHAPTER 42

PARTIES AND SIGNATURES

If you are a party to a contract, then the other party may want to know:
1. Your name
2. Your professional name
3. Your address
4. Your permanent address
5. Your telephone
6. Your social security number
7. Your driver's license (state and number)
8. Your birth date (if you are, or may be, a minor)

The other party may have to fill out government forms in connection with the amount you were paid, and these forms require your social security number. A copy of certain government forms (U.S. Treasury, Internal Revenue Service Form 1099 and Form W-2 B & C) may have to be sent to your address.

You want to make sure who you are dealing with:
1. Club, School, Company, Employer, etc.
2. The printed name of the person signing for the other party: Sugar Rene, Leo Flora, etc.
3. The position the signing person holds: Owner, Partner, Agent, President, Entertainment Director.
4. The U.S. Employer Number.
5. The address and telephone of the Company.
6. The location where you are to do your work.

CHAPTER 43

PAYOLA

Question 1   Does it exist?
Answer 1   *Rumor indicates "Yes."*

Question 2   How is it provided?
Answer 2   *Cash gift. Gift of property. Gift of service. Payment of consideration to a person or company designated by the person bribed.*

Question 3   Why is payola paid?
Answer 3   *The payor wants favored or fair treatment; "favored" in the sense that his records are played or at least considered for pay ahead of other records; "fair" in the sense that his records are played or at least considered for play equally with other payola contributors.*

Question 4   Do some record companies pay radio stations for airtime?
Answer 4   *Yes. Sometimes only spots are bought. Sometimes entire hours are bought. There are other variations.*

Question 5   Is this payola?
Answer 5   *No, not if the time is bought for the rate card amount or off-rate card amount available to other advertisers of the same classifications. However, some companies charge that radio stations prefer records of advertisers to records of non-advertisers during non-purchased time.*

Question 6   Are there laws against payola?
Answer 6   *Yes. Both against the giver and the taker of payola. Also, persons who are caught may lose their jobs and get reputations which may hurt them in attempts to get other jobs.*

CHAPTER 44

PEANUT SIZE RECORD COMPANIES

An artist and his manager decided to take the artist and his well-rehearsed band into a recording studio, to record an album of masters in 6 hours. The LP cover was 2 color; one color ink on another color paper. 1000 LPs were pressed. The artist and his manager were a record company.

The LPs were sold wherever the artist performed and the location was suitable and the promoter was willing. The LPs were sold in record retail stores in the artist's area. When each 1000 LPs were nearly sold out, another 1000 were ordered.

A year later the album cut a second LP. Then the artist and his manager, wearing their record company hats, cut another artist. Each time only 1000 LPs were pressed. A little at a time, the record company grew bigger.

There are a lot of successful, small, local record companies. Some serve small cultural segments of the population (e.g. "Mexican-American" in the Southwest, Greek, etc.). Some serve special audiences addicted to a specific artist or comedian.

Each company, to succeed, must practice activities such as acquiring masters, ordering pressings, getting LPs into stores and other locations, and persuading potential customers to purchase the records.

One record store owner put on one hat as record company and recorded local talent; another hat as wholesaler and placed records in retail stores in the locality; put on another hat as promotion man and persuaded local radio stations to play records featuring local talent; kept his hat as retailer and displayed the records in his store; put on his hat as master producer in peddling the masters to a major record company; put on his hat as manager and booked the band wherever he could; put on his hat as music publisher of the songs in the album and persuaded other artists to record some of the songs. He made money.

The right to use MUSIC from ASCAP'S and BMI's catalogs are granted to:
RADIO and TV Stations—
NIGHT CLUBS—
CONCERT HALLS—
MUSIC BOWLS—
HOTELS—
BACKGROUND MUSIC PRODUCERS & DISTRIBUTORS—
ETC., ETC.

In return, they pay fees to ASCAP & BMI.

(ASCAP & BMI)

THOUSANDS OF SONGWRITERS AND PUBLISHERS GIVE SMALL PERFORMING RIGHTS TO ASCAP AND TO BMI.

In return, they receive payments from these Performing Rights Societies.

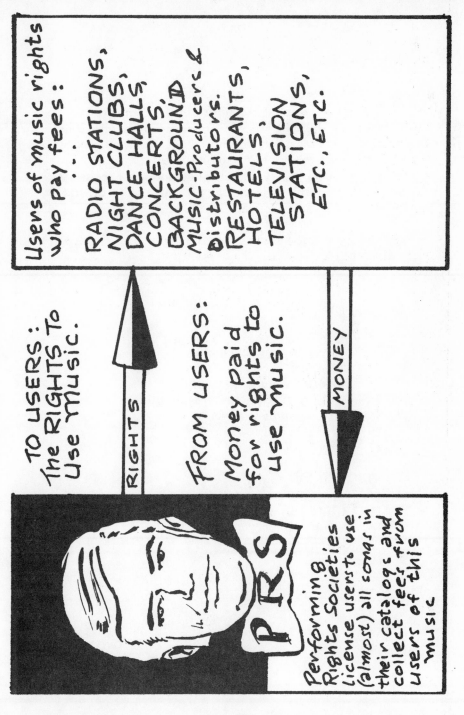

Users of music rights who pay fees:.
RADIO STATIONS, NIGHT CLUBS, DANCE HALLS, CONCERTS, BACKGROUND Music-Producers & Distributors. RESTAURANTS, HOTELS, TELEVISION STATIONS, ETC., ETC.

TO USERS: The RIGHTS To Use Music.

RIGHTS

FROM USERS: Money paid for rights to use music.

MONEY

PRS

Performing Rights Societies license users to use (almost) all songs in their catalogs and collect fees from users of this music

CHAPTER 45

PROMOTERS RATE ACTS

Some acts do their best at performing, others don't. Promoters trade this and other information about acts. The information concerns price; nobody likes to overpay; price varies not only on the act but also on the ability of the respective promoter to pay, on current standing of records as the on the charts, on how much the act wants to work, and how much a promoter wants an act.

Price is only one factor. Promoters don't like no-shows (acts which don't show up). Factors include:

1. Cooperation and attitude
2. Showmanship & professionalism
3. Audience reaction
4. Drawing power
5. Musical accompaniement
6. Performance Start on Time?
7. Performance length
8. Equipment requirement from promoter
9. Act's equipment ready on time
10. Musical backup
11. Arrival as scheduled
12. Agent cooperation
13. Publicity supplied
14. Personal manager cooperation
15. Road Personnel cooperation
16. Price
17. Comments

CHAPTER 46

PROMOTION – TRADE PUBLICATIONS – RADIO STATIONS

PROMOTE
1. The individual record
2. The artist
3. The company

TRADE PUBLICATIONS
1. May publish "news" announcements concerning record releases, signing and recording artists, record selling and release information. This "news" generally comes from publicity releases sent by the record company, the artist, or their respective public relations firms.
2. May publish advertisements concerning the individual record, the artist, the company.
3. May publish news and charts concerning record airplay and sales.
4. May publish additional information in editorials, "who's-doing-what" type columns.

RADIO STATIONS
1. Some person(s) select records which may be played (playlist). Often the disc jockey, working within the playlist, can help a record by playing it as often as allowed and with his ad libs.
2. Different stations have different criteria such as type of music, length of each play, preferrence of single or LP, etc.
3. Selection criteria may be: artist, program mix, particular record, particular company, particular promotion man, particular tastes of selector.
4. Audiences may telephone requests for records.
5. Stores may indicate sales of records.
6. Trade publications may indicate potential success of record in radio station's locality.
7. The record selector may separate records by: (a) recognized name value of record, song or artist and (b) not recognized name value of record, song or artist.
8. Therefore it is important to educate the record selector before he even sees a record which he may select or discard.

9. The record selector may be educated by trade publications (ads, news, columns, charts). Therefore, the record company should try to set the potentially educational material into trade publications.

CHAPTER 47

PROVING EXPENSES

Internal Revenue Service auditors are professionally suspicious that some people are entertainers and songwriters as a hobby (if so, expenses are not deductible) rather than as a business. Many businesses lose money. The mere fact that your business loses money may make the auditor want to say that you are merely operating a hobby.

To help prove that you are operating a business:
1. Keep records of your entertainment activities which make money for you.
2. Keep records of your trying to make more money (e.g., letters of transmittal of songs, contracts, rehearsals, auditions.)
3. Keep your business income and expenses in a checkbook other than the one with which you pay personal expenses.
4. Keep a daily diary. Make business entries each day of business LT (Letters To Others), LF (Letters From Others), TT (Telephone calls To), TF (Telephone calls From). Show where you drove your car, the business reason, the mileage. (Car to Post Office to mail form E etc. for I LOVE YOU TRUE BLUE STU, HIGH AND LOV, Roundtrip 2 miles.)
5. Keep receipts and checks and check stubs and bank statements. Sometimes entertainers who receive cash deposit it in bank accounts, don't report it on the tax returns, and are caught by an Internal Revenue Service auditor.
6. Conduct yourself like a business. For example, what does a business do? It tries to have goods ready to sell, tries to sell the goods to customers. What does a service do? It tries to be ready to render services, tries to render the service to customers. How are you seeking customers?

In your lifetime, your biggest expenses may be: (1) eating, (2) sleeping, (3) transporting, (4) supporting, (5) paying taxes.

Learning more about taxes, and ways of lawfully reducing your outlay for taxes, makes good business sense for every entertainer.

CHAPTER 48

THE PUBLISHER FILES FORM E

Many professional songwriters do not file Form E. They wait to see who the publisher of the song will be, and then the publisher files Form E. These professionals may simply record the song on a cassette, and give the cassette to the publisher. Often a song, as recorded on a cassette, is given to the arranger who arranges the song for an already set artist to record at a phonograph record master recording session. A copy of the song as recorded is given to the LEAD SHEET service, which then prepares the lead sheet.

The music publisher has the LEAD SHEET service or a photocopying service specializing in music manuscript size paper, or a printing service, make copies for the following purposes:

(a) FOR SALE TO THE PUBLIC. There should be a big sign in the publisher's office offering lead sheets for sale to the public for $1 or $2 each.

(b) for the files of the publisher, the performing rights society, foreign sub-publishers, a publisher specializing in printing music, any potential users of the song.

(c) for the Copyright Office (2 copies).

These lead sheets must have the name(s) of the copyright proprietors, the symbol ©, and the year of publication on the title page of the lead sheet.

For example:

© 1975 Suite Seven Music.

We suggest that the lead sheet also use additional information, such as the word "copyright" after the symbol ©, the performing rights affiliation (ASCAP or BMI) after a wide space following the publisher(s)' name(s), the words "All Rights Reserved" because those are magic words for copyright purposes in some Latin American countries.

© Copyright 1975 Suite Seven Music   (ASCAP) All Rights Reserved.

The day on which copies were placed FOR SALE TO THE PUBLIC is important. See the Form E where such information appears.

The name of the copyright claimant on the lead sheet must be identical to the name of the copyright claimant on the Form E.

The letter of transmittal to the Copyright Office from the publisher may state:

Dear Register of Copyrights: Re: I AM LOVEABLE, I AM GREAT, I AM HERE. Enclosed are $6 filing fee, Form E, and 2 copies of the best edition of the music. It is our practice to place copies of lead sheets, such as these copies enclosed herewith, on sale to the public. The date the copies were placed on sale is correctly stated on the enclosed Form E."

Compare the procedure and Form E concerning unpublished music with the procedure and Form E concerning published music.

(Published = placed on sale to the public.)

CHAPTER 49

RECORD COMPANY ARTIST – SELECTION CHECKLIST

1. Is the artist also a talented songwriter?
2. Is all of publishing available for the record company?
3. Is administrative co-publishing available for the record company?
4. Who of the artist group is a necessary member?
5. Who of the artist group should be replaced before signing a long-term contract?
6. Who of the artist group is adequate but unnecessary?
7. Is the group which signs the contract likely to stay together?
8. How long has the group been together?
9. Is the group live performance box office now?
10. Is the group ready to go on the road?
11. How much money paid by the record company will the group need to go on the road?
12. Is this a potential SUPER GROUP?
13. Classification of artist: (Country, Jazz, etc.)
14. Does our record company want to sign an artist in that classification?
15. Is the artist ready to record a single now?
16. Is the artist ready to record an album now?
17. Has the artist furnished (a) demo(s), (b) master(s), which need more work, (c) complete masters?
18. How much front money does the artist want?
19. Has the artist had hits? Which? When? How big?
20. Does the artist have a following? Where? How big?
21. Does the artist have exposure on other media? What exposure?
22. Can the artist go on the road (a) for promotion, (b) as an opening act, (c) as a box office act, (d) a lounge act, (e) a main room act, (f) a main act?
23. Does the artist fit into our company: (a) production, (b) promotion, (c) selling, (d) personality and habits, (e) image.
24. Who in our company "discovered" the artist?
25. Why do we want the artist?
26. How much do we want the artist?

RECORD CO. INCOME FLOW:

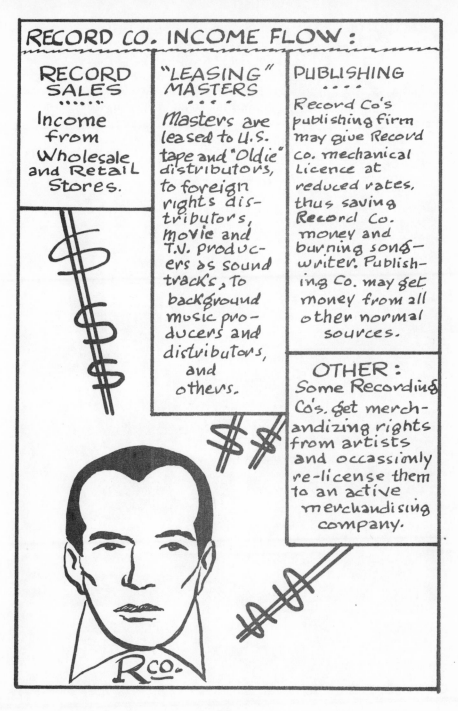

RECORD SALES
......

Income from Wholesale and Retail Stores.

"LEASING" MASTERS
. . . .

Masters are leased to U.S. tape and "Oldie" distributors, to foreign rights distributors, movie and T.V. producers as sound tracks, to background music producers and distributors, and others.

PUBLISHING
. . . .

Record Co's publishing firm may give Record co. mechanical Licence at reduced rates, thus saving Record Co. money and burning songwriter. Publishing Co. may get money from all other normal sources.

OTHER:
Some Recording Co's. get merchandizing rights from artists and occassionly re-license them to an active merchandising company.

RECORD COMPANY PROMOTION DIVISION

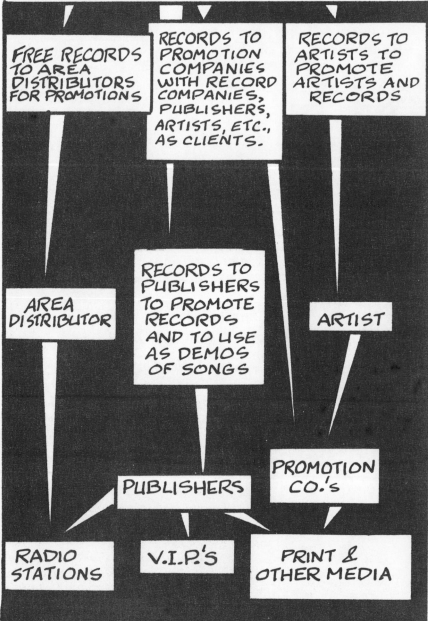

RECORD COMPANIES SALES OUTLETS:

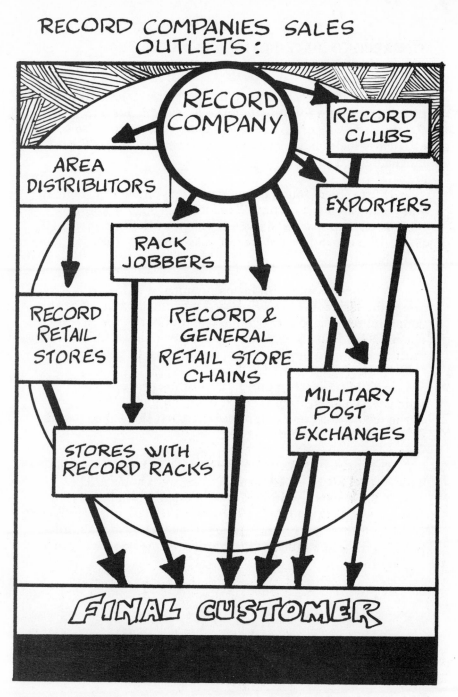

CHAPTER 50

THE RECORD DISTRIBUTION CENTER

Many artists are frustrated by the failure of their respective record companies to keep old releases available for sale. Relatively few record companies concern themselves about efficiently maintaining record distribution centers for slow-moving records.

One problem found by a record company which wants to store and warehouse all unsold records is — space. Problem — records take up space and space costs money. Stored records may cost more money for storage than they might ever bring in.

A second problem in the maintaining of old records for sale is the high cost of meeting each individual order. (Order comes in, the record ordered must be found, the system for placing records in the warehouse has broken down, the record must be packaged properly, the postage must be calculated, etc.)

A third problem in profitably storing, processing and selling warehoused records is just plain ignorance. Those involved in the record company don't know the first thing about using or operating a distribution center.

Please read UNDERSTANDING TODAY'S DISTRIBU- TION CENTER by Ackerman Gardner and Thomas. The Traffic Service Corporation, 815 Washington Building, Washington, D.C. 20005. $10.50. Whether you run your record storage business out of your garage or have enough mail order business to keep a full-time crew business, the book will prove of help to you.

CHAPTER 51

RECORDING
SESSION
BUDGET

	Estimated	Actual	Difference
1. Studio Rental			
2. Tape			
3. Musicians			
4. Cartage & Transportation			
5. Vocalists			
6. AFM fees			
7. AFTRA fees			
8. U.S. Taxes			
9. California Taxes			
10. Use of Licenses			
11. Bookkeeping			
12. Workmen's Compensation			
13. Other			

Each of these items can be broken down further:
For example, Item 1, Studio Rental, may include:

(a) different studios at different times

(b) the same studio on different days of the week or time periods of the day (midnight to 9), 9 to noon, noon to six, six to midnight.

CHAPTER 52

ROYALTY SHRINKAGE

BASIC ROYALTY	Record Companies Promise To Pay Master Producers	Master Producers Promise To Pay Artists
1. US Singles	8% x Retail Price	4% x Retail Price
2. US LPs	8% x Record Replacement List Price	4% x Record Replacement List Price
3. US Tapes Distributed by Record Co.	8% x (Retail − 15% carton cost)	4% x (85% of retail)
4. US Tapes Distributed by Tape Distributor	1/2 of 8% x (Retail −15% carton cost)	1/2 of 4% x (85% of retail)
5. US Budget Line LPs	1/2 of US LPs	1/2 of US LPs
6. US Record Clubs	1/2 of US LPs on 85% of records sold.	1/2 of US LPs on 85% of records sold.
7. US R.C. Bonus Records Freebies, DJ Copies	0% 0%	0% 0%
8. Cut-Outs	0% to 4% x Retail	0% to 2% x Retail
9. Premiums	4% of amount R.C. receives	2% of amount R.C. receives.

BASIC ROYALTY

	Record Companies Promise To Pay Master Producers	Master Producers Promise To Pay Artists
10. Other R.C. income from licenses.	0–50% of R.C. records	0–25% of R.C. records
11. Foreign	1/2 of US	1/2 of US
12. Military / Educational	1/2 or same as US	1/2 or same as US

The percentages here are given only for the sake of example. Most contracts differ in several respects from the above illustration.

CHAPTER 53

SCHEDULING RECORDING STUDIO
PRODUCTION OF A SINGLE

1. Laying down basic rhythm track   3 hours
2. Featured artist(s) sing(s)   2 hours
3. Adding background voices   2 hours
4. Adding strings   3 hours
5. Post-recording editing
       (one hour for each recording hour)

SCHEDULING RECORDING STUDIO
PRODUCTION OF AN LP

1. Laying down basic rhythm track   9 hours
2. Featured artist(s) sing(s)   6 hours
3. Adding background voices   6 hours
4. Adding strings   3 hours
5. Featured artist(s) sing(s) again   3 hours
6. Post-recording editing
       (one hour for each recording hour)

NOTE: These tables are only starting points. Many producers need much more time in the studio, so do many artists, possibly because NEITHER knows what he wants to achieve or how to get there, possibly because he DOES know but the process takes a lot of time.

In the 1950s many hit singles were fully recorded in 3 hours but with the increase of union scale, 8 track, 16 track, 24 track, popularity of groups with record buying followings but without musical educations, recording studio hours increased per single and per album.

CHAPTER 54

SHOULD THE SONGWRITER INSIST ON THE PUBLISHING?

SONGWRITER:
I have written a great song. I insist upon being sole publisher.

RECORDING ARTIST (Alternatives)
1.   *I won't sing the song unless I am the SOLE PUBLISHER.*

2.   *I won't sing the song unless I am the ADMINISTRATIVE PUBLISHER.*

3.   *I won't sing the song unless I am the CO-PUBLISHER. You can be the administrative publisher.*

4.   *I won't sing the song unless you pay me ¼ of the gross amount my record company pays for on your mechanical license covering that song as recorded by me.*

FACTORS: Power of the parties. Fear: will another artist record this song if this artist does not, without the other artist demanding the same conditions?

CHAPTER 55

THE SINGLE

Look at the credits on a 45 r.p.m. "single" phonograph record.

Look at:

1. The name(s) of the songwriter(s).
   Larry Lyricist, Carol Composer
2. The name(s) of the music publisher(s).
   Suite Seven Music
3. The name of the record company.
   Clone Records
4. The name of the recording artists.
   Beet Lover's Fifth Artists
5. The name of the producer.
   Kim Fowley producer
6. The name of the arranger.
   Arene Shall Arranger
7. Next to the name of the publishers, their performance rights affiliation.
   ASCAP (or BMI)
8. The master number.
   MI00IA
9. The record number.
   R 701
10. The length of the song.
    2:20 (2 minutes, 20 seconds)
11. The name of the song.
    I Am Loveable, I Am Great, I Am Here

Behind all this information is the background of many different talents, businesses and legal relationships.

CHAPTER 56

SOLO PERFORMER AND CLUB

If you are a Solo Performer, you can be employed by a Club. Your contract may include provisions such as:

Solo Performer and Club agree:
1. Solo Performer will perform *three* sets of *45* minutes each during the period from 8 PM Saturday (month, day, year) to 2 AM Sunday (month, day, year), the exact starting time of each set to be determined by Club. Solo Performer must be present at Club no later than 7:45 PM.

2. The name, address, city, state, zip, telephone number of Club are: _____

3. The names of Club's employees and their capacities (for example, owner or entertainment director) with whom Solo Performer will deal concerning set times, dressing rooms, credit, pay, and other matters are: _____

4. Club promises to pay Solo Performer:
    (a)   At time of signing this contract $_____
    (b)   Upon appearance at the Club $_____
    (c)   Immediately after the last set $_____
    (d)   Within 3 days after the last performance $_____

5. Club shall: (cross out (a) or (b))
    (a)   Pay the total of the above amount
          as a fee   _____
    (b)   Treat the above figure as a gross salary, and shall withhold appropriate federal and state taxes.

CHAPTER 57

SONG CHECKLIST

Date Checklist Started: _____

1. Song
2. Songwriter(s)   Lyrics
                   Music
3. Date of Songwriter-Publisher Contract
4. Dates of Royalty Periods for which Royalty Statements
   have been sent to Songwriter(s):

_____   _____   _____   _____   _____

_____   _____   _____   _____   _____

5. Dates Mechanical Licenses were granted and to Whom:
   <u>Dates</u>   <u>Artist</u>   <u>Record Company</u>

6. Publisher Song Clearance form sent to ASCAP   _____
                                          BMI   _____
7. Form E (unpublished) date _____
                        Registration No.   _____
8. Form E (published)   date _____
                        Registration No.   _____
9. Form U   date _____
                        Vol. _____ page   _____
10.   WHEN SHOULD FORM R BE FILED?
   _____

11.   Has there been any trouble concerning this song?   _____

CHAPTER 58

SONGWRITER-PUBLISHER CONTRACT

1. The undersigned songwriter(s) represents and warrants that the undersigned SONGWRITER(S) wrote an original musical composition entitled I AM LOVEABLE, I AM GREAT, I AM HERE.

2. The SONGWRITER(S) hereby assign all their rights in said musical composition and its title to the undersigned PUBLISHER.

3. PUBLISHER promises to pay SONGWRITER(S) Fifty (50%) per cent of PUBLISHER's receipts from commercial exploitation of said musical composition from every source except one. PUBLISHER shall pay SONGWRITER no portion of PUBLISHER's receipts from that one source: the performing rights societies (ASCAP, BMI, foreign societies).

4. Royalty statements will be issued for each calendar half-year within 45 days after the respective June 30 and December 31.

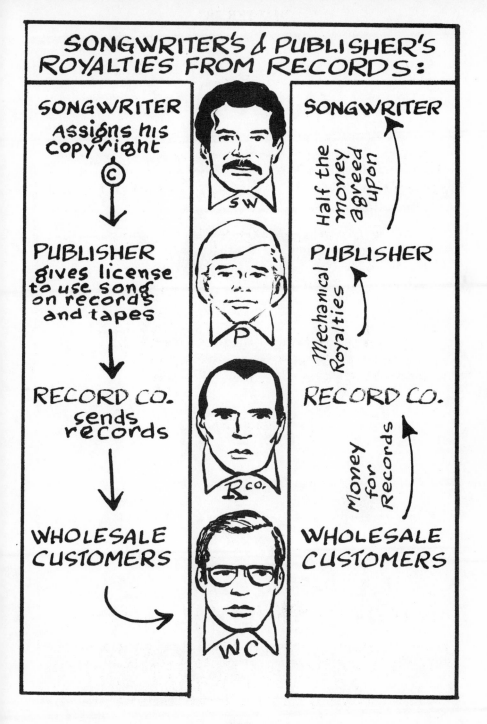

SONGWRITER'S & PUBLISHER'S ROYALTIES FROM RECORDS:

SONGWRITER Assigns his copyright ©

PUBLISHER gives license to use song on records and tapes

RECORD CO. sends records

WHOLESALE CUSTOMERS

SONGWRITER

Half the money agreed upon

PUBLISHER

Mechanical Royalties

RECORD CO.

Money for Records

WHOLESALE CUSTOMERS

SONGWRITER'S INCOME

PUBLISHER'S ADVANCES

ROYALTIES from PUBLISHERS

SW

PERFORMANCE RIGHTS ROYALTIES

Songwriter is paid 50% of Publisher's receipts from mechanicals.

Two Songwriters agree to evenly divide Songwriter's share

CHAPTER 59

STARTING A PUBLISHING COMPANY
— INVENTORY OF FORMS —

1. Songwriter-Publisher Contracts.
2. Letter of transmittal to Songwriter(s) requesting the above contracts are signed and returned to you.
3. Letter of transmittal to Songwriter(s) asking that the copy of the above contract (which has now been signed by you and him) be filed by him.
4. LETTER OF NO ROYALTY to Songwriter indicating that since the previous royalty statement no royalties are due to him.
5. ROYALTY STATEMENT.
6. Letter of transmittal of royalty statement and check.
7. Mechanical LIcense (Publisher-Record Co. Contract).
8. Letter of transmittal to Record Company accompanying mechanical license.
9. Letter to Record Company requesting royalties.
10. 2nd letter to Record Company requesting royalties.
11. BMI form — Writer lists a new song.
12. BMI form — Publisher lists a new song.
13. BMI form — Publisher lists a new recording.
14. ASCAP form — Writer lists a new song.
15. ASCAP form — Publisher lists a new song.
16. Copyright Office — Form E
17. Copyright Office — Form U
18. Letter of transmittal to Copyright Office concerning enclosed two copies of the best edition of the music, Form E, Form U, filing fee.
19. Song Checklist.

CHAPTER 60

STARTING A MUSIC PUBLISHING COMPANY:
JOINING ASCAP OR BMI

1. Get THE PUBLISHERS OFFICE MANUAL by Walter E. Hurst and William Storm Hale: _____
2. Read THE PUBLISHERS OFFICE MANUAL: _____
3. Learn about ASCAP and BMI and decide which of those 2 performing rights societies you will wish to join (a) ASCAP, (b) BMI.
4. Contact that society, and give them 5 possible names under which you wish to do business as a publisher. Usually music publishing companies use the words MUSIC or MUSIC PUBLISHERS or PUBLISHING COMPANY in their names: (a) _____ (b) _____ (c) _____ (d) _____ (e) _____
5. Write down the name approved and reserved by ASCAP: _____
6. Write down the name approved and reserved by BMI: _____
7. Have songwriter-publisher contracts executed by both parties for each song you wish to publish.
8. Grant oral or written permission to record the song(s).
9. Publish the song(s). Make printed music of copies of lead sheets available for purchase to the public.
10. Register your songs with the Copyright Office.
11. File Form U — Notice of use.
12. Grant mechanical license(s) to the record company.
13. Contact the record company to make sure it gives your publishing company proper credit on the label.
14. Obtain copies of the record.
15. Inform the performing right society you want to become a member. (The record label should list your publishing company.)
16. Sign a contract with the performing rights society of your choice.
17. Thereafter, notify your performing rights society about each new song (and if the current rules require it), about each new record.
18. Store that contract very carefully. You may want to quit that performing rights society in the future.

CHAPTER 61

TAX DEDUCTIBLE EXPENSES

1. Office, rehearsal room, storage area are a rent, (or depreciation if you own the building), utilities, business use of home.
2. Telephone and telephone service.
3. Fees to arrangers, copyists.
4. Salaries to band members, equipment handlers.
5. Transportation expenses. Plane, taxis, (depreciation of any car which is owned), insurance, repairs, supplies, gas, oil, washing, parking, repairs.
6. Overnight away from home accommodations (hotel, motel) and food expenses. Baggage fees. Tips.
7. Booking agent.s fees.
8. Manager's fees.
9. Secretarial help.
10. Lawyers' fees.
11. Accountants. Bookkeepers. Tax preparers.
12. Employer taxes, U.S. and state.
13. Workmen's compensation insurance.
14. Office expenses.
15. Trade publications.
16. Membership dues.
17. Coaching.
18. Entertainment. Business gifts.
19. KEOGH Plan contributions.
20. Union + union connected employer contributions.
21. Union membership dues and "taxes."
22. Repairs of instruments and equipment.
23. Issuance of musical instruments and equipment. (No Life insurance is deductible). Car insurance should be grouped with other transportation expenses. Medical insurance should be grouped near other medical expenses. Various insurance expenses are classified differently for tax purposes.
24. Publicity fees, photos.
25. Stamps and postage.
26. Substitutes.
27. Accompanists.
28. Special stage wardrobe not usable for daily ordinary wear.
29. Stage make-up. Hairdos and wigs used for stage purposes.
30. Tips tied in with the business.

31.   Cartage and transportaiton.

32.   Music books, tax books, business books.

33.   Records, tapes, cassettes, sheet music purchased for business (not personal pleasure).

34.   Manuscript paper, ink.

35.   Furniture, carpets, equipment in your office or studio can be depreciated.

36.   Business portion of depreciation items such as television set, hi-fi equipment, radio, tape recorder used for both pleasure and business.

37.   Other items. Analyze each expense you incur, determine whether it helps you in your business in any way.

CHAPTER 62

TEXT QUESTIONS

1. Name 10 record companies.
2. Name 10 recording artists.
3. Name 10 songs.
4. Name 10 songwriters.
5. Name 10 publishers.
6. Name 10 written sources of information on aspects of the record industry.
7. Name 5 songs sung by the same artist.
8. Name 1 song sung by 5 different artists.
9. Define:
   (a) lyricist
   (b) composer
   (c) arranger
   (d) publisher
   (e) entertainer
10. If you wrote a terrific song, and you were an entertainer, would you:
   (a) try to persuade a top entertainer to record your song, or
   (b) would you save the song for your own (as an artist) first record?
11. If you were songwriter-publisher of 5 songs, which you licensed to a record company for 2¢ each for use as an album, and the record company paid you for 150,000 albums, how much income tax would you pay on your gross receipts from the record company if the receipts were all taxed at 50%?

CHAPTER 63

TRADEMARKS

You may wish to give a fictitious name to your group (such as the "Clones"). You may wish to create a unique logo to identify your group (such as ●□●). You may wish to use your fictitious name and logo on your stationery, publicity photographs, advertising, posters, etc. You may wish to file an APPLICATION FOR TRADEMARK REGISTRATION with the Commissioner of Patents, Washington, D.C.

For further information, from the Commissioner, you can write "Please send me forms for use by (a) an individual, (b) a partnership, (c) a corporation, for APPLICATION FOR TRADEMARK REGISTRATION, and please send me instruction booklets."

Also make a notation when you first used your trademark (the fictitious name, OR the combination of the fictitious name and the logo) in intrastate commerce (in your state) _____
date

and in interstate commerce (in another state, too) _____ .
date

CHAPTER 64

TRADE PUBLICATIONS

Trade publications render many different services with their regular (daily, weekly, monthly) issues and their annual trade directories.

Advertisements, editorials, news stories, publicity releases, who's doing what and where, production — promotion — distribution information, what's for sale and where, charts, and other features make the trades important to persons in their respective fields.

Trade publications in the music/record field include, but are not limited to:

1. Billboard
2. Cash Box
3. Daily Variety
4. Hollywood Reporter
5. Music Retailer
6. Record World
7. Weekly Variety
8. Backstage
9. Songwriter's Review
10. Amusement Business

There are many "newsletters," some serving to provide accurate news, others serving as publicity, others providing both news and plugs.

CHAPTER 65

TRAFFIC MANAGEMENT

Consider carefully the amounts of money spent by the music/record industry and companies on transportation of persons, baggage, instrument, equipment, records, tapes, household goods, etc.

Consider the simple question of whether a phonograph record (10¢) should be sent with protective cardboard (1¢) in an envelope (1¢) by 4th class mail (18¢) or by first class mail (about $1.00 — $2.00) with or without an additional special delivery stamp (65¢).

Ask your radio station record selecting friends whether they know whether a record was mailed for 18¢ or for $2.65.

Consider that boxes in which singles are sent come in sizes of 25 records, 50 records, 100 records. A record company salesman who promises a distributor 100 "sold" records and 15 "freebies" creates time consuming problems in the shipping department.

Most record industry people need awareness of transportation issues, answers, ways of saving money.

Read PRACTICAL HANDBOOK OF INDUSTRIAL TRAFFIC MANAGEMENT by Richard C. Colton and Edmund S. Ward. 656 pages including Appendices, Index and Glossary. Heavily illustrated. Published by The Traffic Service Corporation. 815 Washington Building, Washington, D.C. 20005. $21.50.

The book discusses:
"Post office service includes free delivery, but shippers must take packages to the post office at their expense . . . COD shipments . . . Special handling fees . . . Special delivery . . . Insurance . . . Zones . . . U.S. Postal Manual . . . Pamphlets. . ."

Air cargo services . . . Air Parcel Post . . . Air Express . . . Airfreight . . . "Freight routings via air are common and represent a normal way of doing business with shippers of fresh flowers . . .

phonograph records, and other articles the successful marketing and distribution of which depend on the shortest possible transit interval."

Contrast the problems:

(1)   A record in transit is not selling. Cut transit time even though air transportation is more expensive then truck transportation.

(2)   A record which costs too much to move may not be profitable to move.

(3)   Don't overship — a record the area distributor can't move to a retail shop wastes money required to pass the record.

(4)   Don't undership — a release needs widespread sales to rise in the charts.

CHAPTER 66

YOU AS A PERFORMER

If a local location employing entertainers telephoned you and asked you to perform at a concert in one week, would you be ready to appear?

1. Do you sing? Have you learned songs by heart?

2. Do you play instruments? Have you learned songs by heart?

3. Can you read music? Can you at least read chords?

4. Is each instrument ready for use?

5. Is each amplifier ready for use?

6. Is your p.a. (public address) system ready for use?

7. Do you appear with a group?

8. Do you know the full name, address, telephone number, social security number, driver's license information of each member of the group?

CHAPTER 67

YOUR COMPLICATED SHOW BUSINESS LIFE

1. You pay out —
   - (a) For Services
   - (b) For Goods
   - (c) For Use Of Space
   - (d) For Rights

2. You receive payment —
   - (a) For Services
   - (b) For Goods
   - (c) For Use Of Space
   - (d) For Rights

TEST

1. Whom do you pay?
   How much do you pay?
   - (a) For Services (your music teacher)
   - (b) For Goods (a phonograph record)
   - (c) For Use Of Space (your home)
   - (d) For Rights (right to listen to your radio)

2. From whom do you receive pay?
   How much?
   - (a) For Services (for performing at a dance)
   - (b) For Goods (a phonograph record you sell)
   - (c) For Use Of Space (admission tickets to a dance at your home)
   - (d) For Rights (right to perform music at a dance)

You may have read true and fictitious biographies of stars. Did you read about the stars:
   - (a) performing as recording artists for **record companies?**
   - (b) writing **songs** as songwriters?
   - (c) publishing songs in their own **music publishing companies?**
   - (d) producing records featuring **other artists?**
   - (e) performing live on a road tour promoted by a **national promoter?**

(f)   performing live at a **college** or other location?
(g)   retaining **lawyers?**
(h)   hiring **secretaries?**
(i)   staying at **hotels?**
(j)   buying **equipment?**
(k)   owning a **bus** for traveling purposes?
(l)   traveling by **plane?**
(m) being booked by **booking agents?**
(n)   receiving business and career help from **personal managers?**

CHAPTER 68

WHAT ACTIVITIES SIMILAR TO THOSE OF PROFESSIONAL MUSICIANS CAN BE ENGAGED IN BY HIGH SCHOOL AND COLLEGE STUDENTS?

Three of the basic activities are:
1. The musical activities
2. The job obtaining activities
3. The hiring activities.

First: **The musical activities.** They include creation and/or selection of songs and arrangements. Writing arrangements. Learning to play arrangements. Rehearsing. Performing. The musical activities include: making the audience like the musicians.

Second: **The job obtaining activities.** The individual musician auditions for a leader or other selector of musicians who will be given the opportunity of joining the group. The leader and possibly the musicians audition for booking agents to persuade the booking agents to try to book the group. The musicians audition for potential employers (night clubs, tour promoters, concert promoters, record companies). The job obtaining activities include making the employer like the group enough to extend the job and to hire the group in the future.

Third: **The hiring activities.** These are activities which are performed during the entire professional career of a musician by men who must be persuaded that the musician (a) is able to perform the desired job, (b) will perform the desired job. Before each audition or conversation with each person performing hiring activities, the musician should ask himself: "What does the hirer want to see and hear?"

Let's face it. Musically, the young musician leaves a lot to be desired. Yet, often he is hired, while better musicians are not. Why is the musically inferior person hired?

First, because he applied for the gig. Second, because he is willing to work for the financial rewards the hirer is willing to pay. Third, because the hirer believes the musician will show up on time.

Youngsters may work for free, or for $5 per gig, or for any other amount lower than the amount for which a professional musician may wish to work.

High schools and colleges may utilize students in activities concerning band selection, negotiation with booking agents, promotion, advertising, publicity, ticket and poster printing, raising and safeguarding money to promote concerts and from selling tickets.

It is difficult to persuade young performers that they should train themselves for business jobs such as getting jobs and giving jobs (as night clubs, promoters, record companies, etc.).

We'll try.

The lives of entertainers include babyhood, childhood, adolescence (during teen years for most persons, lasting into the thirties for many entertainers), marriage without children, marriage with children and other burdens.

It is at the last mentioned stage (marriage with children and other burdens) that many entertainers want to (a) stop travelling, (b) stay in show business.

A few entertainers can stay in musically creative activities such as arranging, playing in their own restaurants and bars, playing in recording studios. Other entertainers switch to the job-obtaining activities (personal manager, booking agent) or the job-giving activities (TV producers, promoters) or the administrative activities (music publisher).

Each person to whom an entertainer applies for a non-entertaining job wants an employee who has the talent and training to do the required job.

The musician who spent his travelling time meeting promoters and employers, newspaper editors and disc jockeys, learning concert stadiums capacities, strengths, weaknesses, has prepared himself for work in the booking area.

What has this to do with students using their high school and college years to prepare for careers in the music industry?

It is quite possible that the time an entertainer enters the folds of business may occur as soon as the musician leaves school (or even sooner, or very little later).

One youngster became a booker in college and a publisher of a number one record before he could vote.

One youngster who learned he could not sing became a top disc jockey for a top radio station before he needed to shave more than once a week.

CHAPTER 69

WHAT ARE SOME ITEMS ON THE ENTERTAINER'S PREPARATION CHECKLIST?

1. Money to live on until payday
2. Uniforms, change of uniforms
3. Instrument(s)
4. Amplifier(s)
5. Public address system
6. Address book
7. Daily appointment book
8. Box for receipts. Receipt book
9. Written contract executed by the employer for each engagement
10. Road maps
11. Hotel lists
12. Time tables
13. Newspapers (for publicity releases and photographs
14. Copies of records and albums for promotion and sale
15. Photographs for newspapers and for autographing
16. Music (sheet, arrangements, fake books)
17. Car, van, truck
18. Credit cards for gas and car repair
19. Credit cards for hotels, transportation, food
20. Travelers checks
21. Baggage
22. Insurance
23. Musicians
24. Road manager
25. Equipment manager(s)
26. Sample payroll deductions, social security numbers
27. Record distributors' names, addresses, promotion men.
28. Itinerary

CHAPTER 70

WHAT CAN A HIGH SCHOOL OR COLLEGE STUDENT DO TO PREPARE FOR A CAREER?

Let's divide the answer into two divisions:
- (1) during your classes and homework
- (2) the rest of the time

During your classes and homework you can do your best to build several fantastic machines — your mind and your body. By your mind we include your big mouth (so that it can deliver convincing sales pitches) and your fingers (so that they can write and type business like letters of transmittal and publishable publicity releases).

You may protest "I'm a musician. Why do I need to know English grammar, spelling, punctuation, etc.?" You need to know everything since you need publicity (before you can afford to hire publicists), ability to change standard contracts to conform to your requirements, (before you can afford to hire lawyers). You need to acquire a vocabulary so that you can easily absorb new business terms such as contract, guarantee, consideration, right-of-first-refusal, option, cross-collateralization. The difference between a leader (who may be paid twice as much as the ordinary musician) and the musician sideman may have nothing to do with music, but may merely be due to the leader's having mastered the art of communication enough to ask for and arrange the details of a job.

During your classes and homework, please study your tools of trade: your ability to read-and-play, listen-and-play music. Many musicians miss out on the opportunity to become studio musicians because they don't know how to read-and-play music. Please study your instruments so that you can maintain and repair your instruments and those of other musicians (another good source of income). Some musicians have learned to their sorrow that instruments may be damaged while being loaded on or off planes and buses.

During your classes and homework, please study your tools of trade: amplifiers and public address systems. Learn enough to buy well, perform first line field maintenance, spot which troubles you can fix and which you can't.

Other required knowledge:
1. Mathematics (so you can calculate withholding taxes; employers sometimes cheat musicians by withholding too much).
2. Geography (so you can plan one-nighters in such a way that you don't spend unnecessary time and money in traveling between concerts).
3. Etiquette (so you can avoid problems you may create by bad manners; one financial problem you may create for yourself may be due to concert promoter's decision not too hire a rude punk musician again.

College business courses will help you be ready when you try to obtain a business job in the music industry.

One of the amazing lessons of adult life is how much knowledge acquired in school CAN be used many years later.

CHAPTER 71

WHAT DO YOU MEAN BY "WORK ON OPM"?

O.P.M. stands for Other People's Money.

Try to work on "Other People's Money."

First, realize how much money it takes to enable a worker to have tools of trade.

Tools of trade for a musician include:
  (a) Instruments
  (b) Equipment
  (c) Transportation

Kids usually work on O.P.M. which is furnished by parents and various governmental units. O.P.M. is often furnished by employers and by companies which charge fees for the use of their equipment.

1. Study carefully your instruments, equipment and transportation needs.
2. Learn who could satisfy your needs.
3. Figure out how you can persuade these potential sources to actually fulfill your needs.

For example, some instruments seem to suffer no impairment due to age (for example, a bass). You need a bass. Owners of a bass include (a) your school, (b) the music store, (c) your postman, (d) a rich kid who was forced to play a bass for five weeks. Figure out how you can persuade these potential sources to give you the bass for free or for a ridiculously small amount.

Apply the same approaches to your other needs, such as amplifiers, public address system, vans.

Two other sources of O.P.M. are money-lenders and stores which sell on credit.

Money lenders include, theoretically at least, banks, friends, and relatives who love you.

Creditors may or may not wish to give you credit. Academically you may or may not be able to get credit. If you are not able to get credit, can you find some fool willing to let you buy instruments, equipment, transportation, uniforms, etc. on his/her credit?

One professional fool who sometimes allows musicians to use his credit is the masochist called a "personal manager." Being a "personal manager" can be a fun career, with potential rewards of fortune. Personal managers are supposed to "manage" the careers of their clients.

CHAPTER 72

WHAT IS A PERSONAL MANAGER?
WHAT DOES HE DO?

A personal manager is a professional entertainer's "Daddy," who does not have the right to spank his child.

A kid who wants something, and who has a Dad, may ask his Dad to get the something for the kid.

An entertainer who wants something, and who has a personal manager, may ask his personal manager to get the something.

Just like Dad does not (a) try, (b) succeed, every time a kid expresses a want, so may the personal manager not (a) try, (b) succeed, every time an entertainer expresses a want.

One of the things an entertainer wants is a better mouth; the personal manager is supposed to supply the mouth. A musician who constantly praises himself is deemed an obnoxious blowhard; a personal manager who constantly praises his client is deemed a professional.

A personal manager may receive a percentage of the gross earnings of his clients. The percentage may run from ten to twenty-five per cent (depending upon bargaining by the parties). There may be adjustments in the percentage: (a) no percentage of the first $100 per week; (b) no percentage of songwriting or non-show business activities, (c) reduced percentage if a booking agent also receives a percentage.

A personal manager takes a tremendous gamble with his time when he serves a low earning entertainer. Suppose the low earning group earn $100 per night and the manager receives 20%; in such event the manager should receive $20. That sum is very little for a businessman. How much time can he afford to spend to gross $20? Very little. How much money in long distance telephone calls and office overhead can he spend to gross $20? Very little.

The manager aims at bigger money for himself, which he

would gross if the "entertainer" earned more. (The "entertainer" may be an individual, a duo, a group, a whole act, etc.) 20% of $1000 per night is $200. 20% of $10,000 per night is $2000. 20% of $50,000 per night is $10,000.

The manager knows (1) that it takes time to build an act commercially, (2) that he'll be lucky if his client becomes a superstar, (3) that if the client becomes a superstar then the manager wants to cash in on this opportunity of a lifetime, (4) that if the client becomes successful, the client will want to double-cross and dump the manager.

Therefore the manager wants his contract with the entertainer to be a long-term contract, possibly five to seven years.

But the entertainer wants a short-term contract. Therefore he will want TARGET AMOUNTS for each year in the contract, which may list amounts which he wants to achieve as his share of the gross income of the gourp; if a TARGET AMOUNT is not reached in any year, then the entertainer may terminate the contract at the end of the year.

CHAPTER 73

WHAT PUBLICITY, PROMOTION, ADVERTISING SHOULD A LITTLE GUY CONSIDER?

There are people who routinely need entertainers. These people may own or operate restaurants, night clubs, stadiums, dance halls. These people may be entertainment chairmen of social clubs, officer and NCO clubs on military bases, schools and colleges.

Some hirers of talent book the same entertainers each time, or for many weeks at a time. Generally, hirers must keep aware of new entertainers AND of new entertainers who have drawing power.

Entertainers want potential employers to know how to reach the entertainers.

Specific potential employers may be sent photographs, resumes, business cards.

Potential employers may be reached through listings in trade directories or music industry annuals.

Managers often try to persuade artists to pay for advertisements which list the managers' names and addresses. When the artist leaves the manager, the artist may have to advertise extensively so that potential employers learn how to contact the artist.

Advertising pens and letter openers listing the artist's name and address have been used as give-away ads.

Other publicity gimmicks include T shirts containing the artist's name. These may be sold by a representative of the artist at concerts.

Appearances on TV shows (bandstand shows, quiz shows, talk shows) may provide good publicity. Some artists use gimmicks (astrology, cooking, magic, fads), as talk show discussion points.

Some of the best publicity consists of simple one-sentence announcements. ARTIST is appearing nightly at NIGHT CLUB from . . . . . to . . . . for two shows nightly, at 9 PM and 11 PM.

Artists desperately seek one of the best advertisements of all: hit records.

CHAPTER 74

WORKING FOR DISTRIBUTORS AND
RECORD COMPANIES

Record companies hire receptionists, secretaries, shipping clerks, etc. Secretaries are sometimes able to type, take stenographic notes, operate adding machines and photocopy equipment, spell and put up with immature artists and bosses. Shipping clerks are sometimes able to address envelopes and packages, apply postage meters, lift packages, read Post Office and transportation companies' instructions. Record companies also hire or retain advertising personnel, publicity personnel, promotion personnel, selling personnel, bookkeepers, photographers.

Record companies also hire presidents, producers. Sometimes, presidents and producers find financing to create record companies which will hire them as presidents and producers.

BIBLIOGRAPHY
BOOKS

We are believers in books; we read them, write them, collect them. Many people have bought our books for entertainment, education, reference, for themselves and for their staff.

THE RECORD INDUSTRY BOOK ($25.00) introduces the reader to relationships between and activities of songwriters, publishers, artists, producers, record companies; the book contains dozens of contracts which have been used.

THE MUSIC INDUSTRY BOOK ($25.00) explores record promotion, distribution, taxes, careers and contains more contracts.

THE PUBLISHERS OFFICE MANUAL ($25.00) babies the secretary of the publishing firm by instructing her on step-by-step paperwork procedures.

THE U.S. MASTER PRODUCERS & BRITISH MUSIC SCENE BOOK ($25.00) discusses problems of producers, whether or not to lease a master to a bigger company, and covers many uses of music which employ many persons.

THE MANAGERS, ENTERTAINERS & AGENTS BOOK ($35.00) is intended to help people who have the awesome burdens of managing their own and other careers overcome the handicaps of inexperience and ignorance by offering common sense, experience of others, business and legal knowledge.

All these books are published by Seven Arts Press, Inc., 6605 Hollywood Boulevard, Hollywood, CA 90028, U.S.A.

We highly recommend **LEGAL PROTECTION FOR THE CREATIVE MUSICIAN** by Lee Eliot Berk, Boston, Berklee Press.

INDEX

PAGE

SEVEN ARTS PRESS, INC.
6605 Hollywood Blvd. #215   Hollywood, Calif. 90028
ISBN Prefix 0-911370

THE RECORD INDUSTRY BOOK (Stories, Text, Forms Contracts)
Walter E. Hurst & William Storm Hale. Illustrated by Don Rico.
The Entertainment Industry Series, Vol. 1, 1961, 1971. Business and
law book on the record industry. .... Cloth $25.00
ISBN 0-911370-01-3

THE MUSIC INDUSTRY BOOK (Stories, Text, Forms, Contracts)
Walter E. Hurst & William Storm Hale
The Entertainment Industry Series, Vol. 2, 1963. Business and law
book on the music industry. ....Cloth $25.00
ISBN 0-911370-02-1

THE (MUSIC) PUBLISHER'S OFFICE MANUAL (How To Do Your Paper-
work in The Music Publishing Industry)
Walter E. Hurst & William Storm Hale
The Entertainment Industry Series, Vol. 3, 1966. Business and law
book on the music publishing industry. .... Cloth $25.00
ISBN 0-911370-03-X

THE U. S. MASTER PRODUCER'S & BRITISH MUSIC SCENE BOOK
(Stories, Text, Forms, Contracts)
Walter E. Hurst & William Storm Hale
The Entertainment Industry Series, Vol. 4, 1968. Business and law
book on the music industry. .... Cloth $25.00
ISBN 0-911370-04-8

THE MOVIE INDUSTRY BOOK (Stories, Text, Forms, Contracts)
Johnny Minus & William Storm Hale
The Entertainment Industry Series, Vol. 5, 1970. Business and law
book on the movie industry. .... Cloth $35.00
ISBN 0-911370-05-6

THE MANAGERS', ENTERTAINERS, and AGENTS' BOOK (How to Plan,
Plot, Scheme, Learn, Perform, Avoid Dangers and Enjoy Your Career)
Johnny Minus & William Storm Hale. Illustrated by Don Rico.
The Entertainment Industry Series, Vol. 6, 1971. Business and law
book on managers, entertainers and agents. .... Cloth $35.00
ISBN 0-911370-06-4

FILM • TV LAW (Your Introduction to Film • TV Copyright Contracts
And Other Law)
Johnny Minus & William Storm Hale. Illustrated by Don Rico.
The Entertainment Industry Series, Vol. 7, 1973. Business and law
book for film students and professionals. .... Cloth $10.00
ISBN 0-911370-09-9

FILMS SUPERLIST: (20,000) IN THE PUBLIC DOMAIN REFERENCE BOOK
(Over 50,000 Films Listed; Over 20,000 P.D. Films Identified; Sources
Selling Thousands of Films; Copyright and Business Information).
Johnny Minus & William Storm Hale. Illustrated by Don Rico.
The Entertainment Industry Series, Vol. 8, 1973. ...... Cloth $95.00
ISBN 0-911370-10-2